Donald Wesling is Professor of English at
Muir College, University of California, San
Diego. He is the author of *Wordsworth and the
Adequacy of Landscape* (1970), a forthcoming
book of poems, and a biography of John Muir,
the California naturalist.

THE CHANCES OF RHYME

THE CHANCES OF RHYME
Device and Modernity

Donald Wesling

University of California Press
Berkeley   Los Angeles   London

University of California Press
Berkeley and Los Angeles, California
University of California Press, Ltd.
London, England

Library of Congress Cataloging in Publication Data

Wesling, Donald.
   The chances of rhyme.

   Bibliography: p.
   Includes index.
   1. Rhyme 2. English language—Rhyme.
  3. Poetics. I. Title.
  PN1059.R5W4   808.1   78-66016
  ISBN 0-520-03861-4

Summary and Dedication

Idem in sono, in significatione aliud.
The same in sound, two different thoughts at once construed,
By dint of intervening unrhyme separated.
Thus rhyme arrives, surprise, to charge, stress, sing
Our English and to say this book is dedicated
To Judith Elaine Dulinawka Wesling.

CONTENTS

PREFACE

Rhyme, chime. If this be error and upon me proved, I never writ, nor no man ever loved. Plop, plop, fizz, fizz, oh what a relief it is.

Rhymed words leap easily from the page to the ear to the memory. Their mnemonic adhesiveness[1] is such that sometimes it seems impossible to dislodge them from the mind. Their power over us is great and greatly irrational; often the mind's resistance grows in proportion to the ear's delight. That two words with separate meanings should be similar in sound is a transgression of our deepest language habits. In its minor way, rhyme suggests the possibility of solipsism, language pathology, a sound system within language which seems, oddly enough, entirely separate from the ordinary construing of meaning.

Rhyme is a deception all the more suspect because it gives us pleasure. Our suspicion is necessary; our pleasure is real. Both are salutary. This is a book about the relationship of that suspicion to that pleasure.

Let Robert Creeley, a modern American poet who is often not a rhymer, speak of rhyme's continuing fascination for both writer and reader:

Onward then, multiple men, women too, will go with you— boohoo. Which is a poem because I say so, it *rhymes.* That was a primary requisite for years and years. But so lovely when such rhyming, that congruence of sounds which occur in time with sufficient closeness, to resound, echo, and so recall, when *that* moves to delight and intensity, feeling the physical quality of the words' movement with a grace that distorts nothing.[2]

This defense of rhyme is different from the one Samuel Daniel wrote in 1603 as answer to Thomas Campion's allegation that sound-chiming line-ending was, in Campion's words, vulgar, unartificial, easy, rude, barbarous, shifting, sliding, and fat.[3] But the major difference between the two defenses lies not in the reasons Renaissance and Modern offer to justify rhyme; rather it lies in the way Creeley conducts the debate with himself. Rhyme was "a primary requisite," is so no more, and yet "so lovely" it remains. Just barely, Creeley's joy overrides his mocking suspicion of the device that, in a related modern view, "tends to discourage the rediscoveries of essence, primacy, and archetype that are so important to the central impulse of poetry."[4] Modernity is always amazed when, under a certain configuration of technique, a highly traditional poetic artifice so manages words that it "distorts nothing." So rhyme lives on.

It should be clear from context whether by "the device" I mean the status of all devices in the modern era, or the status of rhyme in particular. Usually, rhyme is taken as the surrogate of all other devices, so what is said about the historical situation of rhyme applies as well to meter, metaphor, and other forms of equivalence. By observing how this one form of equivalence is omitted or wrenched, we are able to see with some particularity the kinds of constraints an avant-garde period must enforce upon composition.

Once upon a time poetry was rhyme and numbers, essence defined by format. Some writers and readers, including some who are reading this book, still live within that time. They are my contemporaries; their universe of discourse is neither more nor less cogent than mine. Yet their sense of present possibility is not my own, for I do not require meter and rhyme before I hear poetry. In fact, poetry in any generation is a layered time fabric of anachronisms and parachronisms, time zones running parallel. At a single moment poetic styles unwritable for one readership are current and vital for another. How else could modern traditionalists become aware that in a post-Romantic era their classicism is classicism only in tendency? How else could modern avant-gardists realize the necessity of employing at least some conventions that preexist the poem? Certainly the modern setting is one of multiple perspectives; there is implied conflict between time frames and styles. Within modernity's stylistic pluralism, rhyme still has its way. Yet rhyme has lost centrality, is no longer the very name of poetry.

The historicity of modern poetic style is inscribed within the texts themselves, in their wariness of devices such as rhyme. The degree to which a poem accepts, distorts, or omits rhyme is one rough marker of the extent of the poem's pretensions to being ahead of fad and fashion. Usually the rhyme style can be dated. So, Aristotle to the contrary notwithstanding, there need be no quarrel between history and poetics. A genuine historical poetics may concern itself with the device, as the focus for an inquiry at once chronological and structural.

The foregoing remarks constitute one way of speaking to a larger issue. I have framed certain hypotheses in order to select and describe my examples. I hope that, in general and in particular, the argument will help to clarify how literary texts are made and read in a period that sets unprecedented emphasis on innovation, on spontaneity of action. This book, therefore, is about the ways one traditional art must take its chances in the modern era.

The Chances of Rhyme: Device and Modernity. In this order, the two halves of my title give priority of position to rhyme as subject of most of my pages, and as the most immediately recognizable focus of my study. Perhaps, though, the sequence may forthwith be declared reversible, because this book is only secondarily an account of the phenomenon of rhyme in poetry. The subject of rhyme as device, while not incidental, has really been my way of leading into a set of speculations on some issues in general poetics. With its intent to pose major questions in and through discussions of a technical-prosodic figure, this is thus a small essay on a big subject. The aim has not been definitiveness, which is inappropriate in the present state of poetics. The aim is rather to help prepare the way for a unified field theory by redefining a handful of essential terms, by dissolving certain distinctions and reaffirming others, and by getting down to cases in the analysis and dating of the most representative of all devices. That aim accounts for the general, and somewhat polemical, nature of my Conclusion.

Thanks are due to Andrew Wright for his searching criticisms of drafts of this essay. For other help and advice I would thank John Barrell, Ying-hsiung Chou, Patrick Condon, David Crowne, Thomas Eekman, Willis Jackman, Fredric Jameson, Michael Shapiro, William Tay, Martin Wierschin, Wai-lim Yip, and certain anonymous reviewers. The project has had support from the National Endowment for the Humanities and from the Research Committee of the University of California, San Diego. A slightly different version of the first three sections of chapter three has been published in the Republic of China, and I wish to thank the editor of *Tamkang Review* (Taipei) for permission to reprint.

1: Historical and Structural Coordinates

The definition is, no doubt, the most modest of scholarly genres. Nevertheless, the sharpness and adequacy of critical vocabulary, in a given historical moment, exactly gauges the explanatory power of critical theory.

I begin this study with brief definitions of six related terms in the history of poetic style. Within these terms so defined lies the argument of the following account of rhyme. My little lexicon is itself preparation for a first chapter entirely preparatory. The purpose is to help the reader recognize the complexity of the situation in modern poetry and poetics. With these definitions, really approximations that at once and inevitably involve us in a context of debate, I wish to make explicit for the reader the bias and scope—the poetics if you will—of my argument.

The terms form a cluster; their definitions lean on each other.

Organic form is the first concept. This, or the illusion of it, is what the successful poem has when it justifies the arbitrariness of its technique; and what the failed poem lacks, when its technique seems obtrusively imposed. As applied to the author's presumed compositional process, and to the development of the poem itself, the concept of organic form has been

1

criticized in our day because it imports into poetics a metaphysic that is said to forbid precise analysis; for neither the poet's mind nor the poem's movement can be discussed as structures, if both unite part and whole in the metaphor of growth. Those who see the organic form concept as irrational, reductionist, and a naive evasion of the particulars of poetic structure, like to oppose this notion to the notion of convention. By contrast, I would define organic form as convention in its innovative guise. My view relies, ultimately, on a physiology of consciousness, a sense, as the poet Robert Duncan has it, that mind is shapely and can be trusted to settle into elegant figures. Thus organic form is a calculated overstatement of a literal impossibility: one instance is Walt Whitman extravagantly punning on his very pages as "leaves" of grass. This hyperbole is necessary, because it is the rationale for innovation in the patterning of poetic language. As such, organic form is the primary myth of post-Romantic poetics. Modernity and organic form are born at the same time, and require each other; their origin, at the moment of Romanticism and Coleridgean poetics and methodology, is our moment too.

Rhetoric, the second concept, refers technically to a set of preexisting frames of language, a written or unwritten manual of poetics which proposes to order every present utterance by a patterning of formulae, apt and anterior to the text. Technically, as most critics now know, though they do not always openly concede, language and poetic convention always preexist as a generalized rhetoric, which the poet may not escape but which he may wrench into perceptibility by various, always literary, means. Hence my employment of the term in this wider or more primordial sense. Recent critics have been much interested in formulating a modern rhetoric in this sense, for the description of poetic effects. Rhetoric refers historically to the immense span of time between Aristotle and Quintilian on one end, and Coleridge on the other. Historically, rhetoric as a collective and prescriptive mode came crashing down, and with it the weight of thousands of years of literary precedent, in the first Romantic generation. At the Romantic watershed, for the first time rhetoric is consciously seen as in contradictory connection with what is regarded as poetic.

Modernity, the third term, follows from the other two. It is the historical name for the organicist imperative: everything in the poem, even the prosody, bears the mark of the poet's personality. The ideal of technique as sincerity is an impossible ideal, and yet one that conditions every transaction between the post-Romantic poet and his material resources in language and formal pattern.[1] In poetry under the definitions of modernity, what separates art sentences from ordinary ones is the device, volatile in its position between ordinary and literary language. A certain usage of the device of rhyme, for instance in an otherwise conversational poem by Robert Frost, will produce that kind of justified rhetoric I would call organic form. So modernity must both despise and require the device, and I have tried to give examples of the way this can refresh the reader's attention and, on a larger scale, deflect the direction of the history of literary forms.

Device and *equivalence*, the fourth and fifth terms, are synonyms in the study of specifically poetic forms. All poetic devices, as Roman Jakobson and many others have insisted within the last scholarly generation, are likenings (e.g., in sound, sense, position) of two or more language features. Alliteration, assonance, rhyme, pun, and syntactic parallelism are equivalences of various sorts, but so too are the connections made between tenor and vehicle in metaphor, and the likening of time and stress values in the equal feet of a line of traditional meter. Poetics does not yet possess a general theory of literary language which would subsume and interrelate all these forms of equivalence, showing their several functions when used separately or in concert.

Roman Jakobson has used the term *equivalence* in his definition of the poetic function: "The poetic function projects the principle of equivalence from the axis of selection into the axis of combination."[2] This says that word choice and word sequencing may be distinguished as the relational axes of language: a special interplay of lexis and syntax, of static substitution and temporal concatenation, when language is poetic. Because it is so clearly marked by the ear as an equivalence, rhyme more than meter is poetry's dramatic intersection point of these axes of selection and combination. Not only the rhyme words but also the nature of their separation by otherwise unmarked language is at issue here; my argument shows how each rhyme word has the combined stasis of its emphatic position, and the energy of its trajectory in the sentence, in the line, and in the poem. It follows that any historical changes in this highly marked device, which more boldly even than meter is at once sign and symbol, will result from major shifts in the way poetic sentences and poetic forms are made.

Organic form and rhetoric, modernity and device, are two oppositional pairs, wherein each member of each pair helps explain the other member by the nature of its aversion; I call this relationship a rapport-of-difference. Under rhetoric is its more particular synonym, device; and the next step down is equivalence, a term that describes the parallelism or equating which is the essential structure of all literary devices, a structure varied in each instance of each device.

Rhyme is the chosen instance of a device of equivalence. There exist an indefinite number of purely verbal definitions of rhyme as, for instance, "a repetition of identical or closely similar sounds arranged at regular intervals"; the more difficult task, which this essay attempts, is to indicate the essential history and structure of this device. Verbal definitions can be helpful, though, and I have employed several across the whole possible scale from the linguistic concept of "identical markedness values" (Michael Shapiro) to the deliquescence of the device itself in the general sense that ideas or events may "rhyme" by having similarities of structure or feature.

Rhyme is the boldest form of rhetoric, and perhaps also the most durable, since after Walt Whitman it persistently survives the threat posed to formal verse by free verse, and is employed in free verse more often than most people realize. Even though traditional rhyme is my subject, alliteration and assonance, repeated "figures of sound" (Gerard Manley Hopkins), repeated words and phrases, and *homoeoteleuton* in Aristotle's sense of "making the extreme words of both members of a period like one another" (*Rhetoric*, iii, 9), are all cousinly forms I admit under the title of rhyme.[3] Every variant has its special effect, yet all serve as strong markers of literariness, with the double function of supplying a harmony of sound which is itself beautiful, and of articulating poetic structure by marking off lines and other segments and otherwise acting as the auxiliary of rhythm. Rhyme as sound, as sense, as position all have equal value and space in my account, which has a special concern for the more recent forms of the device. Punning and permutation of language, exact or slightly impaired sound chiming, the same or shifted word position are all instances of the device being remade under new historical conditions.

I hope that when these definitions are placed side-by-side with the ordinary ones they will disestablish a sector of the usual and will be welcomed as clarifying their objects. Organic form has often been summarily dismissed as the assumption that the poem is like a plant growing without the writer's conscious will; so this concept's centrality in post-Romantic poetics, and its subtlety, have rarely been argued. Rhetoric, accordingly, has not been rightly understood as the abominable necessity of our avant-garde era; rhetoric is a repertoire of figures of speech which the organic-form ethos must always tend to avoid, as it tries to render the cut and

curve of experience. To trace the roots of avant-garde modernity in Romanticism is a significant, even fashionable, project
these days, but no explanation has yet taken the account to
the ground level of poetic technique. The terms *device* and
equivalence are tools that enable us to explore the relation of
repetition to sense in the poetic text, leading to observations
on how phonetic repetition plays a rhythmic role. In the
justification of taking any single device, such as rhyme, as a
literary construct, everything depends on the degree to which
this device is (a) treated structurally as the representative formula for all those effects of literary art which are the same
and simultaneously not the same; and (b) treated historically
as one intentional image of poet, period, and original readership.

THE FORM OF HISTORY AND THE HISTORY OF FORM

To speak of history as the reality of a process and not a state,
as something more than ornamental backdrop but other than
proven direct determinant, will widen the range as well as the
precision of poetics. To speak thus clears our way to an
understanding of the poem not as an object but as a practice.

In trying to design fruitful hypotheses that will coordinate
structural and historical accounts of literary texts, I have
found inescapable the need to accept, in the strongest possible
sense, the proposition that Romanticism signaled the major
change in western literary history, inaugurating a new concept of poetic structure.

The chronological premise of this book is that Romanticism, rightly called by Isaiah Berlin the greatest shift in the
consciousness of the west, initiated an epistemological break
in European culture. The later moments known to Anglo-
American criticism as Victorianism, Modernism, and post-
Modernism are based on this premise within the enclave of
Romanticism. Industrialism, mass democracy, historicism,
bourgeois ascendancy, avant-gardism, ethical alienation, and

modernity are synonymous with each other and with Romanticism. The years that have elapsed since 1795 have severely qualified but also deepened the assumptions of the Romantic generation of writers. The moral and formal discoveries of the great Romantics and their gigantic school have yet to be fully understood in history. Whether we like it or not, Romanticism is still the aesthetic and philosophical style of the west.

To my mind, then, modernity and Romanticism are coextensive; and Modernism (roughly 1919–1945) and post-Modernism (roughly 1945 onward) are subparadigm shifts within the larger period concept. Using the terms *modernity* and *modern* to refer to ideas and works after 1795, I deemphasize the lesser, more proximate shift at about 1910. One might use the term *modernist* to refer to technically innovative works after 1910, but never without the sense that modernist writing develops methods in a startling fashion which for the most part originated in the Romantic generation.[4]

The term *break* is, I should admit, a hyperbole for a process that dramatically brought certain persons and ideas, certain ways of making texts, into the foreground. In society as in literature, Romanticism is a speeding up of the processes of style change, an innovation in the sense of being an acceleration.

Matei Calinescu has traced the stages through which the idea of modernity passed before the mid-nineteenth century: from its origins in the Christian Middle Ages, to the Renaissance conviction that "history had a specific direction," to the paradoxes of the modern expressed in Stendahl, Gautier, and especially Baudelaire.[5] Whether or not we agree with Calinescu's contention that artistic modernity proper begins with Baudelaire's programmatic anti-Romanticism, "with its compelling aim of *épater le bourgeois*," Calinescu's main argument is well worth taking as a working hypothesis: "Aesthetic modernity should be understood as a crisis concept involved in a threefold dialectical opposition to tradition, to the modernity of a bourgeois civilization (with its ideals of rationality, utility, progress), and, finally, to itself, insofar as it perceives itself as a new tradition or form of authority." This is valuable because it defines modernity as a concept at once cultural and aesthetic. The term raises difficult issues of social origin and class and ideological affiliation, issues obviously too vast to be resolved in this essay. At this stage in my own argument, it is enough to signal agreement with Calinescu: there is indeed a relation between aesthetic modernity and the modernity of capitalist technology and the business interest. Opposition is one kind of rapport.

Another commentator on modernity, Paul de Man, has argued that through modernity as a term or concept, the distinctive character of literature "becomes manifest as an inability to escape from a condition that is felt to be unbearable."[6] Through modernity understood as "spontaneity of action" and of writing, the literariness of literature can be revealed in all its intricacy. Let us follow de Man in taking literature as an entity that does not "rest at ease in its own self-definition"—so that for us too the distinctive nature of literature is that which is to be defined. We cannot, for example, take it for granted that our scaling down of the legislative force of traditional prosody and rhetoric will remove from any particular device the power and burden of sanctity, and yet to do this will serve to bring to the center of modern poetics the question of the value of formal conventions. From this perspective, the question of literariness or marked language becomes a subset of the apparent contradiction between modernity and history, between spontaneity of action and tradition.

What is the historical character of our post-Romantic moment in which world and language are known to be necessary *but not admitted as such*? Is there a relationship between the

accelerated rate of stylistic change after 1795 and the rapid expansion of a mass public? Is the rise of a whole mode, like a
genre in David Craig's speculation, "likely to occur along
with the rise of a class . . . [and] at a time of social upheaval
and rapid change?"[7] Given the scale of this essay, my answers
must be highly tentative.

My own view is that despite strong traces of a collective
mode in literary practice, which are never lost in verbal
art—which are indeed the condition of existence of any verbal
art—nonetheless, 1795 marks the breakup of formal rhetoric,
the transfiguration of figures. These are implications for
poetic technique of a pronounced shift from a largely collective to a largely individualist mode of writing. That shift had
begun in the very center of Enlightenment practice, yet was
hastened by the events of 1776 and 1789, and actualized by
the writings of Coleridge and Wordsworth in the 1790s.
Seventeen ninety-five is a convenience; plausible as the
literary marker of a wide change that brought in an expan-
ding readership, the bookseller as answer to the patron, a new
straining after public speech just as the relation between the
artist and his consumer was becoming an uneasy one.

Wider still, the change records the emergence and then the
dominance of the bourgeois, in an era of expansion rather
than concentration. The era was one of revolutionary
violence when larger numbers of persons than ever before saw
themselves, for the first time, as in history and making
history. The break, understood in political terms, was a
separation first from the past, which is now seen across the
chasm of political revolutions and the shocks of technological
ones, and second a separation of types of persons, classes
now in relationship each to each as *the others*. History and
human relationships were no longer seen as immemorial and
traditional or chaotic, but were rather informed by those
recognitions of inalienable distance.

The separation between Augustan and Romantic concepts of literary form participates in this epochal shift, by Romanticism's consciously "laying bare," in the Russian Formalist sense as ironic exposure, of all the central Augustan devices. For example, there now arrive on the scene a proliferation of insurgent stress-meters, which accompany a new understanding of genre, syntax, diction, even punctuation. Yet those are surface phenomena. The real change is the move to a stylistic relativism, the absence of any one settled way of writing or organizing, which is the formal aspect of the new period's emergent ethical alienation. Self as voice as style, or what I should call technique as sincerity, is the literary response to a historical moment; the more the public world becomes a mass world, the more the private world is by compensation interiorized: the more a personal voice must seem tangled in the words themselves of the poem.

In this setting the hope to de-emphasize anterior forms grows from a sense that poetry must become more transparent to the world of reference and ordinary language. Partly, the notion of preserving form while seeming to abandon it is an attempt to conquer for poetry some materials known only in "prose" or nonliterature. The extreme overdetermination of the need for interiority in language, the giving of inscape to every tiniest syllable, is a self-protecting resistance of both self and medium to an era that now prizes, more than ever before, univocal understanding, clock time, precise mensuration, and impersonality. A professional practice of literature, put under tremendous pressures by common-sense philosophies and by an antagonistic social order, keeps faith only with difficulty. A literary theory and practice is devised whose sole purpose is continually to thrust to the forefront the notions of reality and ordinary language.

I call this emergent organicist hypothesis the scandal of form. Even in extreme modernism this reality principle prevents the medium from isolating itself from referentiality and speech, from becoming autotelic. Rather than killing poetry by sinking it in form, this habit of mind prefers the risk of sinking it in history, reference, ordinary language, and the existential.

Despite its apparent contradictoriness, the idea of subsuming literariness in the larger world of human experience is today definitive of our era. The contradictions of the idea correspond to those of the era as a whole. In the historical moment when consciousness is divided against itself more than ever before, only certain kinds of poems, certain theories of poems, can flourish; though many other kinds and theories do subsist.

Under modernity's conditions of possibility, dominant theories of poetics—like Coleridge's typical definition of poetry as more than usual emotion and more than usual order—underwrite accounts of the poem which see it as at once conventional and personal, rational and spontaneous. In the realm of technique, this might be shown as a set of contradictory injunctions:

Shape as Superinduced. . . . . Form as Proceeding (Coleridge)
Rhetoric . . . . Style
Positivism in the View of Literary Language . . . .
    Organicist Idealism in the View of Literary Language
Readable or Classical Literature . . . .
    Writeable or Experimental Literature (Roland Barthes)

The expressions in the right-hand column may be regarded as elements in modern literature's surplus of thought beyond the case, the hyperbolical form of common-sense recognitions. Such contradictory thinking is forced on writers who wish to keep an opening of art onto reality *even in the literary medium.* Logically, of course, the right-hand postulates are overstatements and impossibilities, as is the whole of the organicist hypothesis in its pure form. But these postulates are of determining value in the present historical moment, which has not changed its essence despite the coming and going of Victorian and Modern. Anglo-American New Criticism took as its tactic the restating of positions in the left-hand column, the reminder of the absolute necessity of these positions. The next task of poetics would appear to be to explain how and why these positions remain in rapport, necessarily linked; and to show, as the wider part of the subject, that post-Romantic poetry does not accept that self-division is the price we pay for our particular civilization. The present book can only sketch the dimensions of the task, in the belief that whatever its particular viewpoint, whatever its prosodic shape, the intention of our major poetry since Wordsworth is to give images of unified human sensibility. That intention makes a single disciplinary enterprise of the whole period, despite every variegation of polemic and prosodic form.

THE NEW CRITICISM AND THE CONCEPT OF ORGANIC FORM

Under historical conditions of modernity, poetry and commentators are alike meshed in a contradictory structure of thought wherein the highest twin values are the corporeality and the transparency of the medium of language. Poetic form under these conditions is transparent yet insistent, at once a scandal and one of the central issues of post-Romantic poetics. In its ambivalence, the theory of organic form, arguably the most profound discovery of German and English literary Romanticism, gives sufficient justification for opposed belief in both the work's autonomy (its modernity; its transparence) and its position within a web of historical relationships including author, world of reference, and reader.

Organic form as relationship is under attack by classicizing critics who in another phase of their theory adopt organic form as autonomy; and this is their way of being later Romantics. But the New Critics were stealthy Romantics, chastening the Romantic paradigm from within. Hence the rich ironies of their constant struggles against Coleridge, who always returns to subsume their arguments. Hence too the curiosity of their deep resistance to the ideas of intentionality, intersubjectivity, and historicity implied in the concept of organic form, when they had themselves taken over the lesser notion of the poem's self-sufficient wholeness from another phase of the same Romantic paradigm.

Those who are exclusive partisans of an ornamental versification, those who think rhyme the sine qua non of poetry, will find themselves challenged by my arguments. There will be wonderment that a book on a formal device like rhyme should begin by raising the ghost of organic form. And that wonderment will be justified, insofar as an earlier and overstated idea of organic form spoke of poetry as but one conscious phase of the whole of creative activity going on in Nature. Wordsworth and Coleridge were at times lured into this overstatement. Post-Romantic theorists are rightly suspicious of a tendency to dissolve genre and technique into human faculties, bodily processes, and events in the natural world. Yet I shall argue that their concern to eliminate these overstatements prevents them from seeing how Coleridge, for example, keeps in his theory all that is Aristotelian, analytic, and rhetorical, while he promotes also and primarily the new organic concepts of form "as proceeding." Thus they do not entirely see how the concept of the poem as a proceeding is a profound innovation—nothing less than the rediscovery for criticism of the dynamic and unitary qualities of the work of literary art.

Especially in the early phases of the modern outlook we are dealing with the volatile concept of organic vitalism. For this account of text making, argument by analogy is an article of faith; the poem is assimilated to nature. Among human

faculties the most privileged is sincerity, among bodily processes the breath and heartbeat, among natural events the
working of wind and water, and the growth of plants. An-
tagonists of this outlook who are suspicious of organicism
will find their position ably argued by W. K. Wimsatt, who
remarks the difference between saying that our knowledge
reconciles conscious self with nature, and saying "that the
forms of nature are, or are capable of being, suited to moral
reflections—or that the latter can be . . . elicited or superinduced upon the former."[8] It may be doubted, says Wimsatt, if
the theory succeeds in making the transition from general
epistemology to poetics without a leap that "largely abandons
the epistemology as a formal principle." This is a valuable
skepticism to the extent that we may affirm knowledge as
"self-realizing intuition," and poetic form "as proceeding,"
are working principles not provable by writing poems. As
Wimsatt argues, it is impossible to write a poem that will
specially illustrate these transcendental principles.

Yet we must explain why this is so. I think the explanation
is in the diagram of contradictory injunctions already shown
above: Romantic theory emphatically bases itself upon the
gap between visionary principle and particular text. The contradictions to which Wimsatt points are emphatically there,
indeed flaunted; but they are lures enabling innovation rather
than incompletely worked-out theories or crippling confu-
sions.

For the New Critics, organic form in poetry was an untrust-
worthy, even immoral idea, because it seemed to abandon
those preexisting devices that might frame language with
literariness. What the new Critics wanted to praise was this
very literariness, which circumscribed the work as a cosmos
and kept it out of history and ordinary language. The myth of
the poem's autonomy required a complementary myth of its
structure. Hence the centrality of literary conventions and the

need for a heavy investment in the devices of meter and rhyme, those structures that could preserve the poem's sense of integrity. This did indeed evoke splendid descriptions, but often descriptions purchased at the cost of restricting and overspecifying the conditions of literariness.

New Critical premises are most conspicuously Romantic in their adoption of the Coleridgean concept of the single work as organic whole. We are faced here with the powerful historical irony of one kind of organicism, latecoming and diminished, threatened by a larger, more fully dialectical organic vitalism. Like many other English and American critics of his time, and no place more obviously than in his influential essay on "The Intentional Fallacy," Wimsatt applies an organic criterion to the structure and interconnection in the work of art itself, often regarding the work, in W. Jackson Bate's words on a general tendency in New Criticism, as "organic because it is *independent*, with a virtually self-sufficient life of its own." Matching New Critics against Coleridge, Bate asks whether the New Critical "organic approach is sufficiently organic";—whether the unifying principle can exist without a corresponding Coleridgean stress on mimesis, "or the massiveness and significance of the content of experience."[9] In the Coleridgean point of view, which assumes but transforms the classical concept of art as an "imitation" of nature, "a work of art should be organic because it is *dependent* on so many things outside itself, above all on the vital organic character of its subject" (Bate).[10] Sometimes New Critical theory seems determined to defend itself against the world of reference and of history—the world required by the earlier organicism, from which it derives by strict laws of diminishment and reversal. At such times it tries, anachronistically, to judge a creative conception of mimesis by the naive realist terms of the conception Romanticism was attempting to subsume.

Any case for the precision and relevance of the organic hypothesis must expound the meaning of imitation in Coleridgean aesthetics. It is true, as Earl Wasserman declares, that that "'nature,' which once was prior to the poem and available for imitation, now shares with the poem a common origin in the poet's creativity."[11] So we get a mimesis without the cosmic designs that once made it meaningful, an imitation of that which is perceived or felt within the processive structures of the actual world, and a new, autobiographical plenitude with which to fill the hollowed-out concept of Nature. The artist imitates that which is within the thing, not, as in a copy, in the spirit of idle rivalry, but, *natura naturans*, grasping the process of the thing through sympathetic identification. Thus the writer will convey to us his sense of order through the order of his syllables. Here is that interpretation of epistemology and poetics New Critics have missed, for just as the poet, in Coleridge's wonderful phrase, "must eloign himself from nature in order to return to her with full effect,"[12] so also will he use the literariness of the medium to separate himself from ordinary language as a kind of nature.

For Wordsworth, what vitiated Augustan poetic diction was not eloignment but excessive eloignment, an "adulterated phraseology," which over time became "received as a natural language."[13] It was thoroughly characteristic, if unsubtle, of him to claim that the years between *Paradise Lost* and *The Seasons* showed not a single veridical image of outer nature. Not by abolishing but by narrowing the distance of the eloignment, the observable world of reference and history becomes a commonsense test of poetic authenticity; one corrective to Augustan form is nature's endless store of imagery bodied against our senses. "From what I saw with my own eyes, I knew that the imagery was spurious."[14]

In the intensity of developing his poetics of reference, Wordsworth assumes but does not measure the distance from the actual of any language whatever, and he misses the accuracy, the perspicuity of diction in Dryden and Pope. Between his position and Charles Olson's (1950), as follows, the difference is one of tone—not of essence: "ONE PERCEPTION MUST IMMEDIATELY AND DIRECTLY LEAD TO A FURTHER PERCEPTION"; "a thing ought to take off, and put down, and travel at all the varying speeds in between, precisely equal in amount and behavior to the thing it sets out from or seeks."[15] Both Wordsworth and Olson know but leave unstated that poetry is equal to the real but not interchangeable with it. Coleridge puts this best when he says, in "On Poesy or Art," that the fullness of nature is "without character": nature and art require each other to give mutual meaningfulness, the one giving reference and the other giving the signs that make sense of it: "Art would or should be the abridgement of nature."[16] One would only add, as a post-Modern postscript, that we are still very far from a systematic description of the seemingly infinite variety of the abridging process.

After 1795, language comes to be seen as the device both of eloigning and connecting. In the way it contains a rapport within a difference, the Romantic theory of language as enactive secondary modeling system is complementary to those weaker notions, poetry-as-nature and style-as-man. Analyzed into its final terms it is not a facile primitivism, despite those symptomatic wind, water, and plant-growth analogies for mind and style; but rather, at best, a complex tension maintained between cognitive and aesthetic modes, with the text as "a middle quality between a thought and a thing, or . . . the union of that which is nature with that which is exclusively human."[17] If we saw, in Pope, art as "Nature methodized" within the received traditions of writing, in Coleridge we must understand perfect works as "nature humanized"[18] through the agency of coadunative language.

Many issues remain to be worked out in a justification of the concept of organic form. Any complete theory would obviously require a book of its own. That book would probably

attempt to show in detail how Romanticism changed the
received concept of poetic structure. From the Augustan era
when literature is by and large assimilated to all other forms
of learned discourse, we pass, after 1795, to a time when
literature isolates itself. And as the quality of literariness
comes into history, so too does an intense and unprecedented
interest in the conventions that create this quality. The com-
plicating twist in this story comes with our recognition that
after this date the conventions are seen to create but never fully to circumscribe literature. Poetry takes on a life beyond its
techniques, becomes not a substance but an essence. Thence
derives a suspicion of devices like rhyme. I have said that this
story will challenge those who think rhyme the sine qua non;
plainly, on this showing, it also challenges those who despise
rhyme and think it unworkable now.

THE STUDY OF POETIC DEVICES (RHYME IN PARTICULAR)

Rhyme theory shares with writing on versification more
generally the fascination, not in itself irrelevant, with *how a
thing is made*. We choose quotations of bits of poems to
demonstrate a bit of theory, and we choose partially quoted
poems of several periods to make a single structural point
with disregard for chronology; or we make definitions such as
the following, which narrowly restrict the device: "Rhyme is
essentially a kind of stress, and consequently it is found only
in verse that employs a regular stress-pattern."[19] In the handful of book-length studies that have concerned themselves entirely with the subject of rhyme in this century, those by
Viktor Zhirmunski and Thomas Eekman have done well to
discuss the strategies of decanonization which modernity,
more than any previous period, forces upon the inherited
device.[20] An adequate account of the device of rhyme will
consider the meaning of identical word endings; it will then
widen to study the constitution of the line, rhyme-bound seg-

ment, poem; and finally reach out to the question of literary evolution and dating: how does the form (or the signifying absence) of the rhyme stand as an intentional image of a period style, of a particular and specifiable moment in literary history? The attempt must be to shuttle between the structural and the historical inquiries, subsuming the structural in the historical, thus from the start understanding our study of the device as having the dimensions of a general task.

Just such a conception directs Henry Lanz's *Physical Basis of Rime* (1931), a book that nevertheless does not meet all the requirements of a working theory.[21] Employing oscillographs, Lanz makes much of the physical analysis of vowels. It is good to have this evidence, but generalizations from performance are always the weakest sort in prosodic study, because they average out a tiny sample of readings. Moving beyond his structural concerns in his final chapters, Lanz makes a historical survey of rhyming and rhyme theories in the western languages. While this survey is again an important part of our task, in Lanz an immense body of scholarship is at the service of a retrospective poetic canon, defined by a somewhat starved idea of form. Shocked, apparently, by postrevolutionary verses of such as Mayakovsky, and by changes in Russian rhyme, Lanz implies that the renunciation of rhyme is a cause of social unrest.

In the finest essay ever written on rhyme, W. K. Wimsatt takes issue with Lanz's tendency to reduce rhyme to its "physical basis," its sensuous function as separate from meaning.[22] The inquiry of Wimsatt's "One Relation of Rhyme to Reason" (1944) far transcends its marginal pamphleteering purpose, and when I take issue with several of his assumptions, my wish is but to qualify, or to complete. Part of my section on "Rhyme and Reason" conducts a debate with the central thesis of Wimsatt's essay, but here and there this book admits or confirms a number of his secondary points. Like a radiating block of some high-energy material, the densely written Wimsatt essay has many implications for the theory of rhyme and of poetic language.

"One Relation of Rhyme to Reason" is skeptical of Lanz's statistical documentation of the number of vibrations per second possessed by different rhyming vowels. Instead, it restricts its scrutiny to the rhyming of one type of verse structure, the heroic couplet of Alexander Pope. Wimsatt fully acknowledges rhyme's role in batching poetic lines, but he focuses on something less easily identified or exhausted by inquiry: semantic affinities of Pope's rhyme words, the "ironic jostle" or the complementary reinforcement of sense against sense. "The point," he says, "is not to prove that rhyme words must exhibit difference of meaning, but to discuss the value of the difference and to show how a greater degree of difference harmonizes with a certain type of verse structure."[23] He shows that beyond even the identity of sound in Pope's rhymes there is in the rhyme words themselves an inordinately inventive play of association, as well as divergent and convergent meaning. Such verbal play involves words in the same or different grammatical categories, as when verb rhymes with verb, noun with adjective, and so on; but one ascends a scale to rhyme words pitched at different levels of diction, and last to the height of rhyme words linked by a power of associative fusion in the poet's mind. (An instance of this last: In a later essay, Wimsatt speaks of how, in a couplet by Swift, "*Peri Hupsous* gives up a secret through its affinity for 'dupes us.'")[24] Wimsatt defines most clearly the permutations of sound and sense, in their identity and in their difference.

Wimsatt's essay does not limit itself altogether to eighteenth-century examples. It also compares Pope's practice to Chaucer's less witty couplet rhyming, where "lines are all members of a parallel bundle," and where rhymes are less exciting "because the same parts of speech are used in closely parallel functions."[25] By contrast Pope maximizes the possibilities for semantic asymmetry. His practice brings the couplet to the perfect end term of its evolution, doubling the antitheses in chiastic rhyming, "the most brilliant and complex of all the forms of rhyme variation."[26] (Chiasmus is an inversion of the order of words in two corresponding parallel phrases or clauses, or of words when repeated. The best example in Pope of this placing crosswise is in *The Rape of the Lock*: "Where wigs with wigs, with sword-knots sword-knots strive, / Beaux banish beaux, and coaches coaches drive.") The historical axis of the "reason" essay runs from Chaucer through the transcendent Pope to his disciple Byron. However it does not press further to consider the relation of the device to modern practice.

I wrote to Wimsatt to ask why he limited his study to the eighteenth century. In my letter I must have commented on the difficulty of writing on device and modernity, because his reply, dated July 14, 1971, very sharply defended his choice of dealing with the heroic couplet in its highest manifestation:

About my study of rhyme being made "easy" . . . by my choosing to study it in the heroic couplet: Yes, I do nearly always try to study the idea or the phenomenon in full bloom. That seems to me sensible, though doubtless something can be said for studying a thing when it is withered, blighted, or degenerate. I once read an article by an anthropologist down in the Southwest who by a series of plantings had been able to make corn revert to grass, and thus he argued something about the length of time it had taken paleo-Indians to develop their corn. But I don't think he said he was going to take to eating grass. That I think was done by a Babylonian king in the Bible.[27]

While Pope certainly carried the heroic couplet to its highest perfection, critics would probably not be so quick to assent that post-Romantic rhyme is "withered, blighted, or degenerate." On this point, Wimsatt and Lanz seem to agree: for them, one way to gauge the basic nature of modernity is to insist that after a certain moment when "the idea or the phenomenon is in full bloom," all other later products are degenerate.

The eighteenth century is an era of unified period style. The shared social and poetic norms of that time are in essential contrast with the diversity of the Romantic and post-Romantic periods. Yet we cannot conclude that Wimsatt, merely because he supports Augustan ethical and prosodic virtues, is almost two centuries behind the times. Instead, what we need to do is explore another definition of the broad term *modern*, even though our exploration may lead us into seemingly contradictory regions of thought. Wimsatt understands clearly what the term *modern* means and what modernity and modernism are. But in his letter to me and in the points he makes in his essay, he refuses to accept modernity's definition of itself as a culture of rupture. Here I part company with Wimsatt. In my own essay I try to describe, from the avant-garde's own statements, how it uses poetry's most dramatic device. With scarcely concealed delight in recent practice, I will also examine instances of literary and nonliterary rhyming. Thus when Wimsatt opened the subject to philosophical treatment and when he set limits to the discussion, he brought on the pages that follow.

One writer may take the reduced incidence of rhyming as an index of the revolutionary aspirations of a whole historical era; another may argue that any study of one poetic device is too restrictive.[28] Neither of these positions offers an adequate basis for the study of rhyme. Wimsatt's essay is all the evidence we need that focus on the device is valid when the method aptly combines structural and historical descriptions. To emulate Wimsatt's comprehensive approach, while taking the history of rhyme into the nineteenth and twentieth centuries, is to notice a special logical dilemma of the avant-gardist period: while poetry does not now reside in its devices, it is nonetheless impossible without them. Many of the most distinguished writers since 1795 have attempted to cast out the device as the locus of the literary. They have been able to dismiss particular devices, but they have not succeeded in eliminating the general function of literary equivalence. Cast out the choice of rhyme words, their metrical and spatial allocation in the line, for example, and these equivalence functions will be supplanted by others such as meter or metaphor or parallel syntax.

The sentences of art will always put words into a greater field of tension than we will find in ordinary language. The patterns of prosody and of grammar, working together in the poem, combine to increase the amount of information bound language can comprise. "Language," Josephine Miles has written, "means by signs; art means by designs. In literature, signs and designs work together in ways we have yet fully to explore."[29] Because words working together in rhyme entangle form and meaning, rhyme is a privileged instance for such inquiry. Successful rhyme is illogical and canny, striking and familiar, prominent and subsumed; it "provides the condensed formula of poetic language: identity and variation, obligatoriness and freedom, sound and meaning, unity and plurality, texture and structure."[30] While the poem lasts, rhyme designates the reader's acts of attention, that is, has designs upon the reader. Here, then, let rhyme exemplify design.

Rhyme's extreme prominence, often an act of bolder patterning than meter, is, in every line or two, reminding the reader that poetry is a verbal art. Rhyming poetry may seem mysterious in its power to keep the reader's attention, and yet it does overtly flaunt its material basis in the sounds of language. Precisely to cancel the element of *je ne sais quoi* in response to literature, an element that leads to one's reading texts by nonliterary categories, a group was established in Petersburg in 1916 which called itself the Society for the Study of Poetic Language. To discover the internal laws of poetic art, the group began by assuming that "the material of

poetry is neither images nor emotions but words."[31] For members of the society, the proper object of study was the literary
work itself, its own unity and totality as self-defined by the
agency of the device: "If literary scholarship is to become a
discipline, then it must make the literary device its only cham-
pion, for the object of literary scholarship is not literature but
literariness, that is that which makes a given work a work of
literature."[32] The device was not for them an ornament but
the formal principle according to which the work is organized;
they began with the device in order to base their investigation
of the literary fact in the sound stratum of the work. Thus
they started closer to rock-bottom than the Anglo-American
New Critics. The latter did not develop an interest in sound
strategies.

In the initial period, the Russian Formalists, or morpholo-
gists as they preferred to be called, examined the aesthetics of
repetition in simple combinations of sound and sense. Osip
Brik's article on sound repetitions showed how rhyme and
alliteration are particular cases of fundamental laws of
euphony. Later work added a historical dimension. For example, Viktor Zhirmunski's *Rhyme: Its History and Theory*
(1923) described how nineteenth- and twentieth-century
deviations from canonic Russian rhyme produced specific
types of inexact rhyme.[33] Certain aspects of this morphological poetics, still fresh and relatively unexplored even now,
have a bearing on my argument:

1. *The device creates literariness.* "The device . . . , understood as a conscious technique of 'making' a literary work of
art—or shaping its material (language) and of modifying its
subject matter—. . . [is] the key concept. A literary work is
the unity and sum total of artistic devices."[34]

2. *The device focuses attention on the verbal medium.*
"The function of poetry is to indicate the lack of identity between the sign and the object. Why do we need to be reminded

of this? Because being constantly aware of the identity of *signans* and *signatum* we feel at the same time a need or inadequacy: without this fundamental antinomy the connection between a sign and its object would be automatized and the sense of reality would disappear."[35]

3. *The device deploys the sequencing and effect of the poem in the reader's cognition.* The device is the agent of defamiliarization, where the familiar is made to look unfamiliar; of defacilitation, where a special intricacy of language requires more than usual attention to word patterns; and of retardation, where the reader's reception of the poem is slowed down by digressive baffles.

4. *Depending on historical circumstance, the device is used in different ways, either masking itself or calling attention to itself.* There will be times in literary history when the patterning principles of equivalence will need to lose prominence, making literary language seem much more like ordinary language; at other times the device will need to flaunt itself, laying bare the strategy, pointing to its own literariness.

Clearly Russian Formalists assume the uniqueness of literature. They believe that literary language gains its integrity by its separating itself from literary history, psychology, everything extrinsic to the text.

Within these limits the formalists developed unprecedented explanatory adequacy. Theirs was an avant-garde criticism, strong in theory and precisely empirical, and written by persons in close contact with recent developments in the arts, especially poetry. However, as their critics remarked in the twenties and since, their definition of the task tended to rule out coordinates of the highest difficulty and importance. It was impossible for them adequately to pursue the question how the form of a poem is the final articulation of a historical moment of forces.[36] Nor was this possible for the society's survivors—Tynjanov, Shklovsky, and Jakobson for example

—and the historical study of devices remains an assignment
for poetic theory.

The author of a scholarly history of this literary movement,
Victor Erlich, maintains the formalists' work would have
been more solid if they had been less involved with the literary production and local controversies of the postrevolutionary decade.[37] His account thus de-emphasizes the presence of
lines of connection between modernist creation and a synchronic or nonhistorical criticism; but in fact the analytic
mode of this criticism, its way of taking literary language as
an autonomous system, is Russian Formalism's way of living
out modernist imperatives in the sphere of commentary. Russian Formalist criticism, like the New Criticism, takes poetic
technique as its major concern for the same reason that much
modern poetry employs free verse and attempts to assimilate
poetry to nature. We study the device, take it as an object as
Wimsatt does in the title of his book *The Verbal Icon*, because
of our post-Romantic need to play down its significance.
Necessarily, that is, we take literature as an institution, poem
as object, device as verbal icon. But it is the historical fate of a
post-Romantic era profoundly to regret this self-conscious-
ness with respect to the device and to try to circumvent it.
How can literature be less literary, a device less like a device?
Chapter three considers this question. The device in the
modern period achieves the seemingly impossible task of
making a framed and patterned language appear similar to
the run of speech. Chapter two displays successful and failed
rhyme as an extended instance.

Joseph Conrad writes from the center of the modern when
he complains in a letter: "I seem to have lost all *sense* of style
and yet I am haunted, mercilessly haunted by the *necessity* of
style."[38] The device is the bearer of this self-aware style and
thence derives all its historical and structural complexity. The
device is the bearer of a rapport-in-difference; it exists at the

juncture of literary history and modernity, and of literary and ordinary language. Thus:

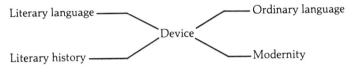

Henceforward my attempt will be to forestall any hopes that we might treat literary language out of its relation to ordinary language, or history out of its relation to the programmatic spontaneity of modernity. In the above schema, ordinary language and modernity are insurgent principles, related to literariness by procedures of reversal or warfare. New works, added to the canon in the post-Romantic period, are very consciously the refreshing of literary language and literary history. In the device, as it has its place in poem and history, the contradictions of language and history are united in experience. The tenets and practice of prosodic avant-gardism show that poets have had this understanding of the device since Coleridge. But the state of theoretical poetics shows that modern scholarship has not caught up with modernist writing. To come closer to the actual choice making, the immersion in cognitive and historical chance, of contemporary practice may seem indecorous. Yet the risk of such an inquiry must be taken by anyone who wants to historicize the precisions of the Society for the Study of Poetic Language.

THE ESSENTIAL UNITY OF LITERARY AND ORDINARY LANGUAGE

Twentieth-century criticism speaks of literary language and ordinary language as though there were two languages. But this is an analytical convenience. There is just one language, which becomes literary by being generated through and by means of conscious constraints.

This is one of those cases in modern poetics where we must perform the unifying operation Coleridge spoke of as *distinguishing without dividing*. Literary history and literary modernity exist as a rapport-within-difference; so do literary language and ordinary language. One of the Russian Formalists, Osip Brik, recognized this essential unity when he proposed as a method for poetics that "Verse language has to be simultaneously understood in terms of its similarities to everyday language as well as in terms of its dissimilarities."[39] The dissimilarities, admittedly, are very striking. Because rhyme seems a departure from the run of speech, we positively avoid rhyme in ordinary speaking and practical writing. Presumably we do so because ordinary language, to keep clear the lines of practical communication, needs to separate itself from the supersaturation of linguistic signals. Rhyming is not efficient; it means extra work for producer and receiver of strings of language. Its extra decorum might even be thought impertinent, a kind of unfair advantage, as if one who rhymed insincerely brought art into talk.

Nonetheless, whether for play or emphasis, nonliterary language does employ its own intricate rhetoric. Rhymelike features, usually discontinuous, are so much a part of the common discourse that they go literally unperceived. Indeed, observation of language habits outside literature suggests English could not do without a sound-linking device that so valuably organizes both language and mind. Echoic families of morphemes have been analyzed by linguists, who challenge us to appreciate the vastness of the "pool of forms interrelated through rime and assonance."[40] The advertisers, debased poets, draw upon this marvelous fraternity of words when they say, "Cadbury's Rhumba, You'll Succumba," or, "Winston tastes good, like a cigarette should." Roman Jakobson has elegantly elaborated the linguistic basis for the success of the slogan, "I like IKE."[41] Still vigorous, Cockney rhyming slang substitutes the rhyming object for the one intended, achieving a discourse, akin to poetry, studded with irrelevant metaphors whose key is not semantic but phonic (for "his plates of meat," understand "his feet").[42] American song lyrics of the 1930s include "Flat-foot floogey with the floy floy," "Who's your little whoozis," and "Jeepers creepers, where'd you get those peepers." Children's jump-rope rhymes enjoy the same phonic surplusage; and after a popular television program every child in every school in England is next day singing a mocking rhyme, "Whistle while you work, Hitler is a twerp."[43] One begins to suspect that, within English, the device is intrinsic, its chances of survival coextensive with the chances of the language itself.

To reverse the direction of the examples and view rhyming from the perspective of literary language, it is clear that literature comes halfway to meet the habits of ordinary speech. Michael Shapiro has recently shown that advances in our understanding of the phonological structure illuminate the study of literary rhyming, and proposed a new definition of rhyme based on equivalence rather than identity:

Rhyme is the regular recurrence in sequentially (syntagmatically) corresponding positions of phonologically (paradigmatically) equivalent sounds, equivalence being expressed in terms of identical markedness values.

This definition has enabled him to claim a special explanatory power in reconciling and subsuming all varieties of "impure" rhyme (assonance, consonance, alliteration, and so on) under, in his words:

a general rubric which qualifies canonic or 'pure' rhyme as a special case, rather than as *terminus a quo*. Phonetic identity, therefore, is not a *sine qua non* either; it is only one of the possible (albeit exceedingly common) ways in which the equivalence principle of rhyme based on phonological markedness is fulfilled.[44]

Thereby language and verbal art are seen as systematic and related, and Shapiro goes on to show how the same markedness values (tense vs. lax, for example) operate as structural principles in Russian folk rhyme and Russian literary verse. Both popular and imaginative verse, in fact, always rely on the reader's recognition of a crucial difference between literary and ordinary language. The humor of commedians who act out a visit to the doctor in limericks, the effect of Molière's brilliant dialogue as deployed in couplets, rely on our perception of the difference between the flow of ordinary speech and the equivalences set up by literary representations of speech. There are schools of acting which radically de-emphasize the rhymes of *Love's Labours Lost*: this means swallowing the rhymes and bringing out in delivery the many effects of movement, enjambment, and breaking off.

Many rhymers wish to shape literary language to give an illusion of tones of conversation. Let me give due emphasis to the speech quality of Robert Frost's "Desert Places" by quoting the whole poem:

> Snow falling and night falling fast, oh, fast
> In a field I looked into going past,
> And the ground almost covered smooth in snow,
> But a few weeds and stubble showing last.
>
> The woods around it have it—it is theirs.
> All animals are smothered in their lairs.
> I am too absent-spirited to count;
> The loneliness includes me unawares.
>
> And lonely as it is, that loneliness
> Will be more lonely ere it will be less—
> A blanker whiteness of benighted snow
> With no expression—nothing to express.
>
> They cannot scare me with their empty spaces
> Between stars—on stars where no human race is.
> I have it in me so much nearer home
> To scare myself with my own desert places.[45]

Rhyme is here one of many patterns of equivalence, and shares with most of the other prominent patterns a certain asymmetrical impairment that helps give the illusion of discursive speech. The first stanza, for example, is not a true sentence but a complex fragment, with loquacious repetition, an intensifying interjection, and speech accents that run counter to the theoretical matrix of the iambic pentameter line (especially line 1, which energizes the utterance). Simple repetition, most of it previous to the end of lines, changes a few letters or perhaps the position of a word, and seems to be meant as a rudimentary form of rhyme:

> *Snow falling* and *night falling*
> *fast*, oh, *fast*
> *around it have it—it*
>
> The *loneliness* includes me unawares
> And *lonely* as it is, that *loneliness*
> *Will be* more *lonely* ere it *will be* less
>
> *no expression—nothing* to *express*
> *Between stars—on stars*
> *myself with my own*

The poem's title similarly returns as its final two words, reproducing this kind of repetition figure in the large and bracketing the whole poem with yet another emphasis. The symmetry of each stanza is impaired by the unrhymed third line, yet the sequence of third lines would seem to set up its own system of sound linkage: lines 3 and 11 end on the identical word "snow," and lines 7 ("count") and 15 ("home") have vowel sounds similar to "snow" (nasals in proximity to the *o* vowel). Line 11, lacking a true rhyme of the sort set up in the first, second, and fourth lines of its own quatrain, has internal rhyme and alliteration as if in compensation. This minor wrenching at the level of the rhyming device reinforces the redundancies of syntax and statement, and metrical stutters like the one in "They cannot scare me with their empty spaces" (where "not" and "me" add two extra insurgent speech stresses to the line). The quantity of impairment is in itself significant. The poem treats the Romantic and High Victorian subject of isolation with a nervous, colloquial form of versification and in an unusual type of quatrain: repudiation of magniloquence in the planned casualness of the technique. A special tone is gained by uttering metaphysical statements in this intimate, genial voice.

The distinction between literary and ordinary language is a useful one. All I am saying with this example is that the tendency to hope the distinction can be narrowed is characteristic of an avant-gardist period. The difference between rhymed and ordinary language may be very remarkable, but the similarity is more important. That is why Gerard Manley Hopkins minimizes the difference while depending on it in his definition of rhyme as "speech wholly or partially repeating the same figure of sound."[46] And it tends to confirm the period dating adopted here to note that Coleridge had arrived at something very like the present book's account of the literary device as early as his *Biographia Literaria* (1817), when he corrected Wordsworth's misstatements on meter and poetic diction. With its organized patterns of equivalence, which even in the most minimal poetry crowd formal-semantic meanings into the line and thus raise language to a higher power, poetic writing concentrates more meaning into itself than we find in practical language. Yet it is not, thereby, another language, a total linguistic system in its own right.

There is a related issue. For too long, literature has been elevated above not only the common language but also the lesser genres. Often, however, nonliterary writing and the lesser or folk genres are dialectically related to literary art, which transforms the details and methods of these other modes. Wimsatt, in his essay on rhyme, implies a scale of complexity and literariness with Pope and Milton at the apex. He prizes the artfulness of intricate verse forms:

The more primitive and forthrightly emotional the poetry, as in balladry, the less it may demand the sensory resistance of verse non-parallel to logic. The more sophisticated and intellectualized the poetry, the more it will demand such resistance.[47]

Wimsatt's statement will be tested by the examples in the following chapters. Many of these examples are selected either from Chinese poetry, where for Western readers the line between sophisticated and emotional is less easy to draw; or from materials that might seem subliterary: jump-rope rhymes, childrens' poetry, competition entries done to order, political rhymes chanted to drums, failied rhymes, as well as the typographical prosodies and distorted rhyme of the most recent poetry. Rudimentary rhyming, unsuccessful rhyming, and avant-garde rhyming have some merit as evidences concerning the relation of rhyme to reason. Popular and intellectualized rhyming practices may be taken as commentary on one another: here too a rapport is to be traced.[48]

Wimsatt's example of the ballad is pertinent. Because the heroic couplet, at the end of Pope's century, lost its ability to carry meaning, Blake, Wordsworth, and Coleridge refreshed poetry by reaching back to the ballad, turning the ballad's tones and stanzas to the purposes of a poetry, at base, scholarly and intellectual. Emily Dickinson discovered her voice in the tiny quatrains and queer rhyming of the hymn (she said she needed the little bells to cool her); and Wilfred Owen found the assonance of his half rhymes in ancient Welsh and contemporary French practice, as well as in the odd off-rhymes earlier English poets used when they could not find perfect ones. Hardy and Frost renew the rhyming quatrain, a form that had been often slack after the triumphant variations of *In Memoriam*. Let these stand as instances of the way the newest forms of rhyme often result from rapprochements between imaginative and popular verse; or between avant-garde and archaic verse, literature and speech. Finally rhymelessness, always the newest fashion in any age, is one possible restorative for a poetry that needs transfusions from vulgar diction and the vigor-inducing syntaxes of prose.[49]

2: Device: Aspects of History and Structure

SYSTEM AND STRUCTURE OF RHYME

When a writer begins to perceive that his need mocks his gear he has already begun the change from versifier to mature poet.[1] In an early letter (1909), Wallace Stevens defines this combined limitation and necessity of the poetic device:

> In the "June Book" I made "breeze" rhyme with "trees," and have never forgiven myself. It is a correct rhyme, of course—but unpardonably "expected." Indeed, none of my rhymes are (most likely) true "instruments of music." The words to be rhymes should not only sound alike, but they should enrich and deepen and enlarge each other, like two harmonious notes.[2]

When the correct device is also the expected one and by definition outworn, the act of composition will bristle with difficulties, with unforgivable wrong choices. The device itself will be parodied, distorted, or avoided in such a way as to make its absence very remarkable. After the "June Book," Stevens tends to avoid end-of-line rhyme because he cannot invariably strike with it the true, unprecedented note. (One result: he becomes arguably the most skillful technician of blank verse since Milton.) During this same, early modernist moment we find Mayakovsky joking:

> Maybe,
>   only a handful
>   of unprecendented rhymes
>   remain undiscovered
>   in Buenos Aires.[3]

Similarly Brecht, in "Bad Times for the Lyric," claims that in his song "A rhyme / Seems . . . presumptuous," and Marianne Moore calls for the allocation of only those rhymes "synonymous with gusto." In the most powerful way, with a new access of technical virtuosity, modernism renews the demand of the Romantic poets: not, or not often, for the abolition of the device but for its highest degree of transparency.

It is statements by the pseudo-avant-garde and the anti-avant-garde which raise the alarm that rhyme is being suppressed in the twentieth century. Acquaintance with the modernist and postmodernist demands for unprecedented rhyme, such as those just quoted, tends to quiet such fears and to confrim T. S. Eliot's more sensible reading of the relation of rhyme to modernity. There is "no campaign against rhyme," Eliot wrote in 1917:

but it is possible that excessive devotion to rhyme has thickened the modern ear. The rejection of rhyme is not a leap at facility; on the contrary it imposes a much severer strain upon the language. When the comforting echo of rhyme is removed, success or failure in the choice of words, in the sentence structure, in the order, is at once more apparent. . . . And this liberation from rhyme might be as well a liberation *of* rhyme. Freed from its exacting task of supporting lame verse, it could be applied with greater effect where most needed.[4]

In the age Eliot helped to define by his practice, rhyme is obligatory only for those unimaginative, unhistorical poets who write advertising copy or squibs on newspaper opinion pages. More than in any previous period, poets know when now to use the device: how to make its absence significant, how to supply its want with other devices of equivalence, or how to turn the rhyme (when it is used) so to avoid the unpardonably expected chime. These technical matters will be discussed, so I need here only reaffirm the level at which Eliot has addressed the question; for his splendid statement contains in germ a theory, to be unfolded here, of frustrated expectation as the motive power of the device in cognition and in history.

Is rhyme gaining or failing? Though the definitive answer would be of some interest, there is no way to provide this needed answer through a priori conceptual reasoning or empirical research. Rhyme, especially at line end, remains the most obvious form of equivalence. In combination with meter, this narrowly defined figure of sound has been the emblem of poetic language since Chaucer. So ingrained is this identity-in-difference of minimal pairs, rhyme has become another term for poetry, just as, in turn, poetry is a surrogate for the human studies more generally, the moral consciousness of the era. This doubtful chain of synechdoche has been the cause of alarm since the early modernist period, in gloomy books and articles which connect the survival of poetry and the humanistic spirit with the survival of rhyme and meter.[5] Yet rhyme has neither gained nor failed, either in the statistical or in the qualitative sense, but simply changed. Preferring not to use the teleological terms *progress* and *degeneration*, I describe rather than judge each historical period's deployment of rhyme. But of course the description is not entirely innocent. Inevitably, because of the predilections imposed by my own history and my understanding of the gaps to be filled in modern poetics, the following historical-structural description of rhyme emphasizes the modern over the traditional, intellectualized over primitive rhyming, success over failure; and yet I try to give more than a little play to the alternative perspectives by bringing them in when I can.

In "The Chances of Rhyme," a poem as yet little known, though it is one of the superlative lyrics of its generation, Charles Tomlinson has written against "all those who confuse the fortuitousness / Of art with something to be met with only / At extremity's brink, reducing thus / Rhyme to a kind of rope's end."[6] Free play, randomness, risk taking in the use of the inherited devices of art, such is the artistic method of an avant-garde era. Tomlinson is right: "To take chances, as to make rhymes / Is human," and such chance taking defines the post-Romantic writer. My argument extends Tomlinson's theory of art and specifies further meanings for his title. I take the chances of rhyme to be in the first instance historical: the possibility of innovating the device in a period suspicious of all conventions. How did we come to a state of affairs at which a poet wants every rhyme to be his own invention, inscaped and selved? That meaning I call *system*, referring to the way poets choose to relate rhyming schemas to concepts of genre and decorum in a given period (e.g., satire seems to require clipped couplets). There is also an ahistorical meaning: the cognitive unpredictability of the device in its effect on the reader. How put a blade of logic between the rhyme-paired words to determine their degree of seamlessness and surprise? That meaning I call *structure*, referring to the sequences of acts of attention of writer and reader as these meet in a poem. These two notions of system and structure direct the inquiry as coordinative definitions.

A SHORT HISTORY OF RHYME IN ENGLISH

"And thou in this shalt find thy *monument* / When tyrants' crests and tombs of brass are *spent*" (Shakespeare). Rhyme in English requires that two or more positioned words have the same vowel sound in the last stressed syllable: with different sound features preceding, the same sound features following that vowel. That last sentence is as much as a prosodic manual might want to say about the device, and yet there is more to say, albeit speculative, about the semantic relationship between rhyming units, about the early desynonymization of language (no doubt a fiction) which the device seems to imply. The discovery of a rhyme argues, that is, the human limitation of language, its dispersal into separated sounds and meanings, and its lucky economies when, as J. S. Schütze said of rhyme in 1802, two meanings find the same sound.[7] Might the rhyming words be related, somehow, in convergent meaning as well as similar sound? Some have wondered: Wimsatt, Hugh Kenner, and John Hollander have written on the phenomenon of semantic convergence of rhyme words; a linguist describes families of rhyming words; in a recent poem with rhymes of a planned randomness, Charles Tomlinson says that the chances of rhyme are "like the chances of meeting— / In the finding fortuitous, but once found, binding."[8] That difference-in-identity of minimal pairs, batched at measurable intervals, creates a principle of cognitive eventfulness —except in rhymes like "proved-loved," Shakespearean, automatic, thereby strictly unworkable. (This is not to deny that "proved" and "loved" had a quite exact pairing of vowel sounds in the pronunciation of Shakespeare's time.) These extinct rhymes evoke not expectation but perceptual automatism in the reader, and I have called them Shakespearean as a rough way of suggesting that a poem's defeat of automatism —its making strange of theme and rhythm—is successful in cognition only because of a prior act of historical imagination. Bad rhyming comes of following routes closed off by literary history: not knowing what is prosodically possible in a given period, thus mistaking archaism for innovation. Examples follow in this chapter.

My study of device and modernity centers on the rhyming practice of the past quarter century in England and America. It hopes to subsume the knowledge of the whole history of the device which recent usage inevitably implies. (For the effective tradition at this moment is what we know of the tradition.) My version of recent poets' knowledge of tradition follows in this section; my aim in undertaking this history of rhyme is to understand the origins of the present state of affairs where rhyme is no longer an appropriate synechdoche for the poetic fact. Richardson, Saintsbury, Lanz, and Pendlebury have performed the history of the progress of the device through traditionally defined period styles, usually associated with centuries.[9] Now that we may rely on their valuable work, it is time for another history of the device. My survey describes a process that, within my own terms of reference (learned from such as Tynjanov and Shklovsky), constitutes literary innovation: namely, the era-by-era exposure of the device as a device. I shall not often describe how the device is abandoned, though that of course happens on occasion; rather I hope to show how a literary group or generation, or a single great writer in his or her work, regains the ability to use the device at will. Writers, so I argue, do this by unmasking the device, showing it to be merely what it is, and thereby dispensable. There is an objection to doing history in this fashion: it can be said that we find in the period previous to the epistemological-prosodic break evidences that prefigure an avant-garde intelligence, seeing thus, in the past, only ourselves. One response is that only after the epistemological break, and by virtue of its emergent historicism, are we able —with interpretive categories of some strength—to segment processes of change and variation before Romanticism.

Rhyme, a device of bold patterning, is an instance of that "shape as superinduced" Coleridge opposed to "form as proceeding." Its use in a given period will be a test of reigning conventions of traditional shapeliness. This has not always been recognized. The presence of a valid unrhyming verse since Whitman makes necessary, in fact, a form of history of the device which refuses to take the device as a neutral object.[10] There is no time in the history of rhyme when this device was not a matter of contention, whether in practice or in prosodic theory. There are conflicting poetics of rhyming and rhymelessness, or of one type of rhyming as against another. Usually the debate is between different sectors of a period's writers, but occasionally—as with Campion, Milton, Auden—one finds it in the work of a single writer. Incipiently the debate is present in any writer's work, and if one cares to look for them, there are hints of a fit of rhyme against rhyme in nearly every poet. Such contention seems necessary to the historical continuance of the device.

In a rhyme-rich language like Italian, there is perhaps too much that is unpardonably expected, so with major writers like Montale and Quasimodo, rhyme comes into very great disrepute. English is not rhyme poor: the code of the language permits and encourages rhyme, and yet imposes strict and conventional limits on the range of likely homophony. For example, it seems rhymes of the "prove-love" variety come into currency only by tacit agreement of writers needing the resource and willing to permit "eye rhymes" into the canon.[11] Around this device, as around all others, there has developed a structure of convenient fictions which define its expressive capacities in a given period. These fictions can to some extent be specified. To compile a nearly complete record of prominent devices and their use in the present century would require voluminous quotation but would satisfy our craving for an explicit poetics. In the absence of such a document, and lacking any explanation from linguists as to why some literatures like Spanish or Old French can employ terminal assonance instead of rhyme, it seems imprudent to keep calling rhyme the differentia of prose and verse. This way of thinking is very likely another venerable convenience twentieth century practice has brought into doubt; and yet any account of the origin and use of rhyme in English must show the essential descriptive-normative role of such a concept up to the generation of Whitman, and indeed beyond. There are reasons for believing that far from being merely the "stub" of the line, as Vladimir Nabokov maintains,[12] end rhyme since its first use has constituted the line and its meters. If in traditional verse, rhyme and meter have in fact interanimated each other, it follows that without rhyme, lines will be built up and recognized by other methods, metrical and grammatical.

Though study of the sound systems of texts would yield good returns in any account of total meaning, we still lack a persuasive notation for the effects of sound which, even in mental performance, characterize the most intimate and speaking elements of a poet's verbal art.[13] No wonder some still maintain seriously that rhyme is merely ornamental, an effect unrelated to meter, and that in any text sound is subordinate to sense. Again, because rhyme is still, in Harold Whitehall's words, "the most mysterious of all the sound patterns,"[14] it is considered by many the unanalyzable quintessential feature—the most representative feature. Rhyme is seen both as absolutely detachable from and absolutely the essence of poetry. Such contradictory attitudes derive partly from the traditional mistaken notion that rhyme is not intrinsic to the line, an altogether simpler item than meter and therefore a diversion from the essentials of prosodic study.[15]

In part, too, the difficulties are inherent in the device itself and its origins. Rhyme is, says Whitehall, "non-indigenous to most European literatures, and has apparently been acquired by us from some South Mid-Asian Semitic language by the process of acculturation."[16] Rhyme was not a boldly prominent organizing feature in the ancient classical poetry of the West, and this fact conditioned its emergence in the modern vernaculars. The purely theoretical ictus of Greek and Latin quantitative prosodies was apparently a disincentive to rhyme. "As long as stress was ignored in verse, modern rhyme, which depends on it, was obviously impossible; it is recurrence of stress, not verse-ictus, which is needed for rhyme."[17] The real beginnings of rhyme as we understand it, "harmonizing with stress-accent and supporting the rhythm of the verse, are to be found in the tenth century"[18]—in Latin hymns, then vernacular hymns and leonine hexameters. So the deep harmony of rhyme enters Europe at the same time as organized Christianity.

Since stressing and rhyming emerge in history at the same time, very likely in symbiotic relation, there is no prima facie reason to believe that rhyme has any less part in the constitution of the line than meter. "Nations who unite prose accent and arsis," according to one student of Latin hymns, "need to mark off their verses plainly. They do it by rhyme, the rhythmical repetition of letters."[19] Now Georges Lote, the historian of French versification, says that rhyme in French as in Latin was "merely a means of helping syllabism by marking the end of the line."[20] But even in a syllable-count measure like that of French, if rhyme marks the line's end, it must not merely help, it must constitute such a measure; meter, a principle of infinite expansiveness, cannot (in the period after classical prosody and before blank verse) *brake itself*. Lote admits as much, I think, when he remarks that in medieval hymns, rhyme "is a means of marking the end of the line in a way which would strike the ears of the hearers indifferent to quantity and to an accent of which the music took no account." If the hymnological hypothesis is correct, rhyme moves from Latin to the vernaculars in such a way as to implicate its end-marking function with the rhythm and syntax of the rest of the line. Perhaps, then, the end of the poetic line properly begins at the line's beginning.

Rhyme was destined to be more emphatic in English than in French because of its adding, upon the privileged position of last stress, the added prominence of harmonious sound. Perhaps with the lack of a regular principle of stress, French has from the start been less able to justify, or at least to emphasize, its rhymes; poetry in French reacted far more decisively than poetry in English to the early modernist war on devices, and now the fifty-year ban on rhyming and on syllable-counting measures seems to have become a simple condition of creation. From the language of Racine, of Baudelaire, rhyme has more or less faded away as a literary device—perhaps for cultural reasons, perhaps because of the lack of a supporting principle of metrical stress. The device has been more tenacious in the language that received it as the result of French conquest.

There is not, as the result of Norman invasion, of change in the culture and language of England, of church domination of Europe, of the rise of vernaculars, any contention over the device of rhyme: this is the time of its establishment. Yet rhyme is very much an issue between the existing alliterative poetries in the native tradition and the end-rhyming poetries on the French-Italian model, which are emulated in the dominant dialect by Chaucer, for of course rhyme had existed in fraternal forms before the tenth century. In Old Saxon, Icelandic, and Anglo-Saxon, alliteration was structural, other rhyme incidental. Possibly the frenchification of English meant a movement of accent toward the end of words, or at least a diminishing of initial accent, making words more suitable for terminal-syllable rhyme. Despite the use of alliteration till the end of the fifteenth century in the North and West, rhyme on the last syllable of the last word becomes the norm in English since Chaucer. Assuming a social and literary superiority, Chaucer at least once mocks gently the alliterative verse of the provinces, and yet he also supplies in "Sir Thopas" a whole tale that exhibits the full range of ineptness in tail-rhyme verse (*rime couée*).[21] Chaucer once explicitly complains about the "scarcity of rhyme" in English, and elsewhere admits that now and then his lines "fail of a syllable." A recently deflectionalized language must sometimes have been difficult to rhyme into, and not even Chaucer could give English a display of virtuosity like the Provençal *canzon* or an intricate carrying metric like Dante's *terza rima*.

By writing in dominant-dialect English, with the end rhymes of Jean de Meun and Dante, Chaucer set the pattern of urbane literature for centuries. And yet end rhyme was but one of several possibilities when Chaucer had just begun writing. The more various rhyme—rhyme in other places than the line end—seems to have been lost from the home-grown European literatures after end rhyme became the norm. Henry Lanz, a historian of this period's rhymes, rightly says that rhymes "gravitate toward rhythmically important places,"[22] but he overemphasizes the line end as the line's critical spot. Beginnings and middles can be "ends" too, when they are breaking points of rhythm and syntax. Before the consolidation of end rhyme in the vernaculars, rhyming effects seem to have been more various and inventive than at any time since. The variegated usage of the past fifty years in English raises some doubt, at least, whether end rhyme is really the evolved and predestined highest form.

I am describing a moment of paradigm crisis and uncertainty. A poetic device fostered by the church in its hymns, and brought from France, is gaining influence over a strictly indigenous related device. For a time the two overlap, until the insurgent device takes over. The coexistence is also a form of debate, though never aggressively argued. Indeed so cordial are the relations between the differing prosodies, that on occasion they are employed in the same poem—either in the same line, as in *Pearl*, or in different parts of the same alliterative stanza, as here in *Sir Gawain and the Green Knight* (ca. 1350–1390):

> An oþer noyse full newe neȝed biliue,
> þat þe lude myȝt haf leue liflode;
> For vneþe watz þe noyce not a whyle sesed,
> And þe fyrst cource in þe court kyndely serued,
> þer hales in at þe halle dor an aghlich mayster,
> On þe most on þe molde on mesure hyghe;
> Fro þe swyre to þe swange so sware and so þik,
> And his lyndes and his lymes so longe and so grete,
> Half etayn in erde I hope þat he were,
> Bot mon most I algate mynn hym to bene,
> And þat þe myriest in his muckel þat myȝt ride;

For of bak and of brest al were his bodi sturne,
Both his wombe and his wast were worthily smale,
And alle his fetures fol3ande, in forme þat he hade,
    ful clene;
For wonder of his hwe men hade,
Set in his semblaunt sene;
He ferde as freke were fade,
And oueral enker-grene.[23]

The long lines in the body of the stanza are alliterative, but these modulate into the clipped lines of the closural "bob and wheel," also alliterative but rhymed as well. This wonderful stanza makes special use of its rhymes: the huge knight is first introduced and described here, making his entry into the poem; his most startling attribute, his color ("hwe"), reserved for the last word of the last line, clinched in with a startling rhyme ("oueral enker-grene," "entirely *bright-green*"). These intermediate forms of great beauty, as reinvented in the alliterative-rhyming verse of Gerard Manley Hopkins, suggest that certain prosodic resources remain in our stock of forms, genuine but dormant.

After a time when Skelton's exuberant chain rhyming of short lines seems the most interesting usage, if not the most characteristic, the device of rhyme is exploited in many of its possibilities.[24] Wyatt and the English Petrarchans of the early sixteenth century take special interest in rhyme as a tool for weaving together different lengths and quantities of lines. Now enters in prosodic theory, on the basis of an already remarkable achievement since Chaucer, the belief by Puttenham and Sidney and others that English "before any vulgar language . . . is fit for both sorts" of poetry, quantitative and accentual, unrhymed and rhymed (Sidney, *Apology for Poetry*). Rhyme was, in fact, the one sweet new form of equivalence which the vernaculars had added to poetry (though Puttenham, searching precedents, recalls that some literatures before the Greek employed rhyme). So it was argued, except by those diehards who wished to expose the device because it had no classical sanctions and because, so they felt, it went against the very grain of the language. The antagonism against rhyme was in its origins a theoretical position, a nobly conservative and classical scholasticism in such writers as Theodore Drant, Roger Ascham, Spenser's correspondent Gabriel Harvey, and Richard Stanyhurst in his perverse translation of Virgil (1582). But the antagonism was also local and contemporary, in the sense that Elizabethan opponents of rhyme wanted to raise the dignity of English by shaping verse in elevated quantitative measures and were embarrassed at the pinchbeck chiming of rhymed verse. Yet after the 1570s antirhyme sentiment persisted into the era of the most magnificent flowering of rhymed poetry: deep dissatisfaction with rhyme was manifest in the development of dramatic blank verse and in the antirhyme essay and unrhymed lyrics of Thomas Campion. That Campion was, like Milton, a masterly rhymer, is not to the point. What interests is the need to expose the device and the polemical practice of the exposure, for these by an irony of history make a classicizing scholar-poet, Campion, one justification for prosodic experiment in the twentieth century. William Carlos Williams, especially, has admired Campion's pugnacious example, his search for rhymeless measures.[25]

In the next phase of this history, the quarrel shifts from quantitative verse against rhyme to blank verse against rhyme. The curious violence of Milton's famous preface to *Paradise Lost* and his development of a flexible medium of blank verse for Christian drama and epic are the most notable features of the period after Campion. Yet others in different ways are plainly dissatisfied with the rhyming poetry of the period 1603–1660. Ben Jonson has "A Fit of Rime Against Rime":

> He that first invented thee,
> May his joynts tormented bee,
>   Cramp'd forever;

Still may syllables jarre with time,
Still may reason warre with rime,
        Resting never.[26]

The metaphysical poets, from Donne through Marvell, arrange unpredictable rhymes on taut, uneven-length lines; Abraham Cowley writes carefully asymmetrical stanzas in his influential Pindar translations of 1656; and we have in Richard Crashaw an amazing scheme of pet rhymes, where the poet exposes the device by working up his own system of rhyme-word associations, reusing rhymes as personal symbols.[27]

The success of Shakespeare and Milton, both as rhymers and unrhymers, became for later generations a dilemma. The rhymed poetry was so various and rich as to make it strictly inimitable, while the great unrhymed achievement was in itself a sustained critique of rhyme. ("Milton, the unrhymer, / singing among / the rest . . . / like a Communist," shows William Carlos Williams identifying with yet another prosodic rebel.)[28] Those conscious latecomers, the English Augustans, found a solution of authority and elegance. For forty years and more on either side of 1700 there was agreement that, thenceforth and forever, literary innovation meant repetition and correction of existing forms and genres. This was, of course, part of a project to fix the language of all communication: vocabulary, orthography, prosody. Exposure of literary devices, like all innovation, is now defined as correction; and the device of rhyme, used so wantonly by Elizabethans, will now be tamed and resolved into couplets. By that form of selective history which enables all poets to evoke their talent and protect a literary identity, the new style finds its precedents not in Donne or Shakespeare or Milton, but in Denham and Waller. Rhyme itself is not abolished, but merely renovated by regulation.[29] In the first (and perhaps last) explicitly written poetics which has legislative force,

Edward Bysshe's *Art of English Poetry* (1702), permissible homophones are described, and, as an aid to writers, the appendix consists of one of the earliest rhyming dictionaries. Also the distances between rhymes, both of sound and position, are prescribed. Sound repetitions are to come at stated intervals, like perfect chimes: any unpredictability of sense or sound would be "harsh," or "rough," an uncivil prosody. Rhyme has of course its illogical, bardic or gothic element, perhaps most evident when it is used as the vehicle of a laughing irony. So for the Augustans there is all the more reason for controlling a device that—they perceived with restrained regret—was not present in the classical poetries they loved and translated. They had this dangerous device by precedent and it was not to be expunged, and so on the one hand they pretended rhyme was completely natural, assuming couplets were the mind's true order and discouraging other styles; on the other hand they controlled the device with the constraints of number and elision in the syllable-counted heroic line, avoiding similar parts of speech at rhyme position. Couplet rhyme, until the death of Dr. Johnson is, then, a peak of achievement gained by determined restriction. It is the emblem of vanquished difficulty and controlled violence.[30]

The period style of English neoclassicism, from the start, was challenged in its uniformitarian prosody by Miltonic writers (Thomson, Cowper), Pindaric writers (Cowley, West, Gray), biblical writers (Smart), bardic writers (Gray, Blake), Spenserians (Shenstone), and balladeers (Percy, Chatterton). In the final quarter of the eighteenth century the heroic couplet seems a trick used by all, but used badly. No one comes to rescue the form or, after Johnson's death in 1784, to defend it in theory. The couplet seems increasingly inappropriate for the new meditative, topographical, or lyrical modes, and its decline, relative to the flourishing of the insurgent types just mentioned, helps to force a major prosodic break just before 1800. With the poems collected in *Lyrical Ballads*, the couplet

is devalued, and rhyme becomes one among several prominent devices, no longer the central device. So just when
emphatic accent comes to modify strict syllable counting in
the meters of poetry, rhyme loses its priority—and loses accordingly all blame for illogical, punlike disturbances of the
semantic table of values. Very few explicit statements about
rhyme are made by the Romantics, who accept it as part of a
vast, complex inheritance. But they accept it on their own
terms, since unlike their immediate predecessors they actively
register the conventionality of the convention. Accepting the
truth that rhyme is soaked in usage, their practice stipulates
that, so far as possible, rhyme must express the very speaking
tones of the writer. One thinks of the complexity of feeling in
Coleridge's simple ballad stanzas; or one remembers the
exuberant sound repetition, unthinkable a generation before,
of Southey's poem imitating (through rhyme) "The Falls of
Lodore"; or Shelley's decision to go for speed in terza rima,
Keats's density in the sonnet or in the richly worked Spenser-
ian and ode stanzas. Realizing that rhyme is a product of history, not of nature, the Romantics reinvent existing forms
with a fine sense of how the device is limited and enabled by
previous work: Keats goes to Dryden to get the sort of couplet he wants in "Lamia," Byron to Pope for the slangy tones of
"English Bards and Scotch Reviewers." After the break at
1795, such a reinvention of the device, like its avoidance or its
use in experiments, will of necessity express some degree of
personal meaning. An unconscionable demand is made on the
device, but one our major poets can tolerate: for over 180
years they have produced a highly conscious poetry in
accordance with this demand.

In philosophy the historical break meant a shift from uniformitarian to diversitarian thinking, in critical theory a shift
from mimetic to organic theories of the poem. In prosody the
couplet gave way to a reshuffling of genres and to stylistic
pluralism. After Wordsworth, and increasingly after Whitman, rhyme and rhymelessness coexist. In the work, for

example, of Wordsworth, Tennyson, Eliot, Auden, Lowell, Ted Hughes, rhymeless verse is abundant, yet these poets are best known as rhymers. Roy Fuller, a scrupulous rhymer for over thirty years, has published *New Poems* (1968) without a single rhyme, apparently seeking alternative constraints; while Edward Dorn, a poet very different from Fuller, whose early work is unrhymed in the school of Whitman and Charles Olson, has written wittily deformed rhyming quatrains as part of his long poem, *Slinger* (1975). Like the editorial decision to divide the poems of D. H. Lawrence by outer form into rhyming and nonrhyming sections, these are typical events in a period of pluralism. Poets now know that only when conventions are recognized as historically developed devices can they be used to the fullest extent as personal language. For these reasons, free verse, which displays modernity's exposure of the rhyme device in the fullest way, has by no means abandoned rhyme; free verse of merit has perhaps used rhyme as densely as many types of more traditional writing. Charles Olson has denounced rhyme in his essay "Projective Verse" (1950), but often in poems he relies on calculated deformations of the device. In fact, since Wordsworth, rhyme is not consciously a fighting issue on the part of those writers who have given it over as a legislative convention. Disputes will arise only when those who wish to prescribe rhyme for all poetry encounter the Romantic need to use poetic devices to throw a light on the conventionality of devices. We have seen how earlier eras have felt a similar need, but never so intensely, never as an organicist premise at or near the center of a whole literary culture.

RHYME AND REASON

More than in any previous age, post-Romantic rhyming is successful when it surprises. If earlier, in his *Essay on Criticism*, Alexander Pope could say that "True ease in writing comes from art, not chance, / As those move easiest who have learned to dance," now the act and art of writing are pretended away, the skill of fitting together left unmentioned. So the poem appears a run of ordinary sentences, though with continual reminders from the structure of equivalences that it is art after all. The reader is led—only half-wittingly as it were—to the point of rest: the whole poem is preparation—not fully perceived till the end—for its own closure.[31] The effect of the post-Romantic rhyming poem is at once casual and calculated, sensuous and logical.

However, just as the art sentences that employ rhyme avoid the marks of labor and resemble talk, so do we tend, with ordinary speech, to neglect consideration of the very sounds of the device which constitute it. Analysis of poetry has been strongly weighted, from the start, toward effects of logic, meaning, and sense: admittedly these effects follow the line of least resistance. The lack of a strong notation for sound repetitions indicates a disinclination to go beyond the signified to the actual verbal signifier and its special aural character; this in turn suggests that such "defections from the semantic system," as Roland Barthes calls rhyme, "cannot be directly explained by means of that system."[32] Apparently the world of sound, with its elusive interior economy, is irreducible: interiority, says W. J. Ong in his essay proposing "A Dialectic of Aural and Objective Correlatives," cannot be resolved in terms of surfaces.[33] For this reason post-Romantic poets and their readers do not share the confidence of most linguists that literariness inheres in prominent stylistic devices. Even the "impersonal" theories of poetry, so characteristic of the period from Matthew Arnold to Eliot and the New Critics, must finally assume the device will be reinvented from within in order to convey personal speech. The post-Romantic poem either resists or reinvents the rhetoric which has existed before the poem's creation. That is the poem's way of protesting its fate of being taken as an object, its way of enacting in advance the aural correlative.

It would appear that students have come at the device either by way of sound or by way of logic, but not with the combined perspective of form and sense together. Roman Jakobson does well to ask if there is a semantic propinquity to match the oral one: "Although rhyme by definition is based on regular recurrence of equivalent phonemes or phonetic groups, it would be an unsound oversimplification to treat rhyme merely from the standpoint of sound. Rhyme necessarily involves the semantic relationship between rhyming units."[34] Below, demonstrating that one main meaning of rhyme involves the permutation of positioned sounds, I follow Jakobson by drawing out the implications of a statement he quotes from Gerard Manley Hopkins, who described the principle of verse as "speech wholly or partially repeating the same figure of sound." Before taking up permutation and position, I want to consider the limitations that follow any decision to treat rhyme mainly from the standpoint of sense.

An early description of the elements of sound may be found in Hegel.[35] Rhyme, he noted, emerged in the European vernaculars just when Christianity became institutionalized on a large scale, a time when language became more intimate and soulful in the Latin hymn. Rhyme was instrument of a new meaning, a meaning of the personal part of the text. By a migration of forms the rhyme device supplanted, in the modern languages, that which was the poetic part of poetry in the classics. According to Hegel, the decay of the quantitative principle made it necessary for writers to find another sort of equivalence:

If the quantitative principle is renounced, and yet despite of it, but in accordance with the necessary demand of art, the sensuous medium is permitted to retain a certain force of resistance as against the exclusive assertion of ideal content, . . . there remains no other means left at our disposal save the express and artificially modulated sound of articulate speech as such.[36]

The sound of rhyme is "speech as such": in art speech the sensuous element, the very breathing and pronouncing, is brought to the foreground of the reader's attention. With any poetic device there will inevitably be a "certain force of resistance" because the look and sound of patterned words emphasizes the material quality of language. Rhymes will be to some extent separable in analysis from the paraphrasable (or "ideal") content of the poem that employs them. If we resist any separation of rhyme from poem, of rhyme from line, we do so, I imagine, because at the final stage of ideal content, the relationship of signifier and signified will have been dissolved. There will exist at that thinkable but perhaps never realizable extreme, as Hegel plainly saw, not a text but a chunk of pure rhetoric.

Hegel's sentence is quoted by Henry Lanz, but in a context that changes its dialectical form into a polemical defense of a sound function "which is largely indifferent to meaning":

In ordinary speech, in prose, we entirely forget about the physical existence of words as signs or sounds. Meaning, ideas, is what we *get for* it. With their physical reality forgotten . . . the words become transparent . . . fully resolved into what they mean. Poetry is called upon to save the physical element of words and bring it to our attention in the name of art. For art and beauty require visible or audible forms through which the ideas may shine. Thus sound, the music of words, acquires an independent artistic value which is largely indifferent to the meaning or sense of it. Therefore Hegel writes [the sentence quoted above]. For rhyme is a means of increasing the sensuous intensity of words in contrast to their logical meaning.[37]

Hegel, though, has not said specific sense does not matter, has not said the "signified" is in any way independent or irrelevant. Nor does Hegel offer warrant for figures of salvation ("save the physical element") or of translucence ("through which the ideas may shine"). Indeed, as I have shown, the whole period since Wordsworth and Hegel is unhappy that literary form may be in some degree institutional, indifferent to the speaker's meaning and personal voice. Literature, of course, would not exist or be recognized as such without semiautonomous systems or signifiers, generic or formal shapes that can be transmitted from period to period, conventions that can be taught like artistic "languages." Nevertheless, while our literature would acknowledge that Ferdinand de Saussure's division of language into signifier and signified is itself a post-Romantic instrument of precision and discovery, our literature must also despise the artificiality of that separation. To note this reluctant dualism is to describe the essential modernity of the era beginning in 1795.

In a recent argument similar to Hegel's, Sigurd Burckhardt (1956) has noted the radical difference between words and the media of other arts: clay, marble, pigment, tones. Language, the poet's material cause, is already a medium before he starts to fashion it—though, says Burckhardt, a medium that "lacks all corporeality": the linguistic signs have only a "secondary, referential substance" since they are tokens of "real" things. Words

already have what the artist first wants to give them—meaning—and fatally lack what he needs in order to shape them—body. I propose that the nature and primary function of the most important poetic devices—especially rhyme, meter, and metaphor—is to release words in some measure from their bondage to meaning, their purely referential role, and to give or restore to them the corporeality which a true medium needs. To attain the position of creative sovereignty over matter, the poet must first of all reduce language to something resembling a material. He can never do so completely, only proximately. But he can—and this is his first task—drive a wedge between words and their meanings, lessen as much as possible their designatory force and thereby inhibit our all too ready flight from them to the things they point to.[38]

Unquestionably. I only emphasize that different periods understand differently this "dissociative" or "divestive" function of poetic devices. Usually eighteenth-century poets preferred the least possible dissociation: they wished to regulate strictly the inherited devices of rhyme and meter, and to circumscribe metaphor. Puns and by extension rhymes, says

Burckhardt, deny "the meaningfulness of words and so call into question the genuineness of the linguistic currency on which the social order depends." In a time when the word as sign has an immense primacy over the word as entity, rhyme is harnessed and the pun falls into disrepute. Since 1795 there has been no comparable attempt to restrict the subversive, independent-of-things nature of the language medium; rather an exaggeration of it, almost a logomimesis.

Until 1795, rhetoric and poetic were (or seemed) coextensive—at no time more purely (and precariously) than in Augustan prosody and poetic diction. Since the shift at that time, when classical rhetoric and the mimetic theory of the poem were not abandoned but subsumed, devices have been understood not as deep structures of the mind but as historical, volatile, the *perpetuum mobile* of literature in the sense that they are reinvented again after lapses of time. It has become one of the tasks of modern poetics to explain how the inevitable device helps a writer achieve a voice, a style, literariness itself, while under different conditions the same world of signs, once saturated in personality, must deprive poetic identity insofar as it preexists the poem's making and saying.

In his study of rhyme, Wimsatt has set himself the task of explaining the icon quality of poetic speech, which would make language into a material. Unwilling to let the device escape control of conscious reason, Wimsatt argues the primacy of sense in poetry. His aim, he says, is to develop the idea that sound features are the effects and outer signs of reasonable-logical determinants, the idea "that verse in general, and more particularly rhyme, make their special contribution to poetic structure in virtue of a studiously and accurately semantic character. They impose upon the logical pattern of expressed argument a kind of fixative counter-pattern of alogical implication."[39] For Wimsatt, sound patterns are not detachable ornaments; nonetheless, they are strictly secondary in logic: "The art of words is an intellectual art, and the emotions of poetry are simultaneous with conceptions and largely induced through the medium of conceptions. In literary art only the wedding of the alogical with the logical gives the former an aesthetic value." Accordingly, this argument considers the semantic element foundational.

One willingly grants to Wimsatt that the cognitive elements in the poem can exist without the aesthetic elements, while the opposite cannot be true in verbal art. The cognitive elements are the sine qua non, the "fixative" of the poem's sensuous materials. It does not, however, follow from this that the poem's meaning has chronological or logical priority. If the sensuous element, the physical words tangled in their literary patterns of equivalence, were absent, the logical element of the poem would be neither aesthetic nor even thinkable. If the discourse is to be literary each is the precondition of the other.

Very apt in this context is Craig La Drière's statement that "it is hard to say whether meanings or sounds more often initiate the poetic process, but there is no theoretical reason to suppose the primacy of either. The great fact is that, once the process is begun, all the elements have a priori equality."[40] Is the sensuous body of language, as it appears in poems, nonlogical? Does the logical function remain unmodified by the physical shape and sound of the words? Can we trust the testimony of poets who say that chanced-upon rhymes have led them to unforseen semantic routes? I do not know the answers, but would agree with La Drière that we can "learn a great deal more than we now know about structures of meaning from the study of structures of sound."

My point is that, quite possibly, Wimsatt's position obscures rather than defines a working concept of literary style. Entering the debate as an antagonist of Lanz's caricature of Hegel, Wimsatt argues that rhyme is a nonlogical device, a device that gives language an unavoidable solidity, a feature it may not deserve. He is not happy with the possible equality

of sense and sensuousness in poetry, and that is why his preferred form of rhyme is the Augustan couplet, a form that reduced to the minimum (a glorious minimum!) all that was
nonlogical and unpredictable. Insofar as Wimsatt's position
affords an answer to Hegel, it proposes a reversion to pre-
Hegelian theory and practice.

Having noted that English prosodists have little to say
about the semantics of rhyme words (the usual emphasis is
not on sense but on degree of likeness of sound), Wimsatt
praises the Popian wit of those couplets "where different parts
of speech rhyme in parallel lines." Rhymes using the same
part of speech in parallel functions, as in Chaucer's noun-
noun rhyme of "bokeler" with "daggere," he calls, by contrast, "tame rhymes," minimum rhyme, "only one step from
homoeoteleuton." Now homoeoteleuton, or the presence of
like endings that are not set out into verse lines, is an ancient
category for the description of effects in prose; by developing
this unwieldy term's implications, Wimsatt here maintains
that "the difference between prose and verse is the difference
between homoeoteleuton and rhyme." In another essay,
"Rhetoric and Poems," this opposition of homoeoteleuton
and rhyme is called "one of the most profound of rhetorical
differences."[41] In this aesthetic system, the distinction between prose and poetry is not one of essence, for poetry
merely superadds a certain repertoire of devices. Yet paradoxically the kind of poetry most like prose turns out to be
norm for all poetic rhyming.

Wimsatt finds Pope's versification the highest type of
rhyming in English, the most complexly logical, especially in
"chiastic rhyme, the most brilliant and complex of all the
forms of rhyme variation." Doubtless the rhyming of noun
with verb, pronoun with adverb, and the like, makes the
reader work hard. The optimum instance of the theory, however, may not be Pope but Ogden Nash. Whether homoeoteleuton is so rudimentary a device as Wimsatt says, whether it
is a prose device strictly, and whether its difference from

rhyme is "profound," are also matters for debate and inquiry. He finds "mere homoeoteleuton" in Chaucer and Byron. Their poetic practice, leading up to and then away from optimum rhyme in Pope, would be closer to prose. Pope's optimum rhyme is a specially poetic writing, for Wimsatt, because more reasonable, in a definition of reason as semantic unlikeness.

Since I want to show that one sort of reason resides in effects of simple repetition, I would question the inference Wimsatt draws with the use of such terms as "mere" and "complex," the inference that homoeoteleuton is neither complex nor literary. With a meagre definition of sensory resistance as semantic unlikeness, he writes: "The more primitive and forthrightly emotional the poetry, the less it may demand the sensory resistance of verse nonparallel to logic. The more sophisticated and intellectualized the poetry, the more it will demand such resistance." Yet a great deal of poetry does not seem to fit these statements about poetic patterning. In ballads there is the refrain; in sestinas, the repeated end word; in villanelles and triolets, the recurring whole line; in Whitman's free verse, anaphora, the repeated line beginning; in American Indian poetry, the hypnotic repetition of words and phrases, a "rhyming" of thoughts and not of words. Wimsatt says rhyme of the highest sort repeats just the final syllable or syllables of last words that are semantically unlike; there must not be complete identity of exact repetition. He has defined his subject of study narrowly as one relation of a rhyme to a reason, disallowing homoeoteleuton as valid poetic device for the same reason that some persons object to blank verse and free verse, the relative absence of bold traditional patterning, of pronounced norm and variation. Homoeoteleuton he thinks to be without a norm; that is the meaning of his adjective *mere*.

Wimsatt, by intention, leaves out consideration of a positional difference, yet difference of placement does offer a perfectly complex alternate norm in post-Romantic poetry. The same word in a different place has not all the same poetic aura. Exact repetition is in fact a variety of equivalence, not phonetic (though sound is involved) but locational. Homoeoteleuton, in its modern varieties, is in this account a variety of rhyme broadly defined, neither more nor less sophisticated than any other sort of rhyme. It is one kind of poetic device, neither more nor less "reasonable" than any other, with a special effect that depends on the way the poet sets out the poem and the way the reader takes it in.

Like Wimsatt, I should reassert the equal importance of the sensory and logical functions of rhyme. Yet in his special emphasis on the logical function, making it foundational, he at some points in the argument underestimates every other variety of rhyme before and after the time of Pope. Consider the parallelism and antithesis in this passage from Randall Jarrell's "A Well-To-Do Invalid," where the figure of sound is indeed a figure of logic, yet we have no conventional end rhymes whatever:

> When you first introduced me to your nurse
> I thought, "She's like your wife." I mean, I thought:
> "She's like your nurse—" it was your wife.
>
> She gave this old friend of her husband's
> A pale ingratiating smile; we talked
> And she agreed with me about everything.
> I thought: "She's quite agreeable."
> You gave a pleased laugh—you were feeling good.
>
> She laughed and agreed with you.
>   I said to her
> —that is, I didn't say to her: "You liar!"[42]

The whole poem (in which the nurse-wife dies first, leaving the invalid "well with grief") is a textbook instance of the relations of parallelism to reason. Repetition is its organizing principle, and the enabling rhetoric of its ironies, for every return of a significant word or phrase undercuts the first utterance. "Her dishonesty is so transparent / It has about it a kind of honesty." Semantic likes, suffering perhaps here and there the slight permutation of an added prefix, withdraw everything given, in a sustained fit of cruel reasoning. The effect is sly. It is gained by homoeoteleuton.

In free verse and the prose poem, with their unspecified ends and middles, there is far less obvious pattern than in conventionally rhymed poetry. But equivalences are not absent. Neither Pope nor W. K. Wimsatt would, I suspect, approve the extreme measures taken in Mallarmé's "Un Coup de dés," whose unit is not the word or line or even the page, but the foldout. One must imagine the binding fold running down the center:

COMME SI

> *Une insinuation*   *simple*
>   *au silence*   *enroulée avec ironie*
>   *ou*
>   *le mystère*
>   *précipité*
>   *hurlé*
>
> *dans quelque proche*   *tourbillon d'hilarité et d'horreur*
>   *voltige*   *autour du gouffre*   *sans le joncher*
>   *ni fuir*
>   *et en berce le vierge indice*
>
>   *COMME SI*[43]

Top left and bottom right this "unit" is bracketed by the "COMME SI" phrases ("as if"); and viewed as a whole resembles a feather, or quill pen as image of the poet's labor. Temporary, fleeting rhymes ("en berce le vierge") are brushed by as the passage finds no completion but rather syntactical and metaphysical suspension of the second "COMME SI." The mind works over a large body of syntax to get down to that second "as if," which is at once a pause and a promise of more to come in the poem's movement, over the page. The chances of rhyme, of repetition of any sort, are fragile in such a setting, and yet they are there, in the play of like-sounding syllables ("précipité-hurlé"), and in the upper case of the bracketing phrases. Tipping down and right, the page foldout resists visual balance. The two "COMME SI" phrases are transitional, leaving the vast stanzalike page open at either end in syntax and logic. Rhymelike this instance of exact repetition performs the musical and logical functions of rhyme, over a distance of syntax which may well be forbidding, but then Mallarmé is hoping to extend the mind's cognitive powers with new patterns of pagination, white spacing, sentencing, and sounding.

Dylan Thomas gives no such help in his (superficially more approachable) introductory poem in *Collected Poems* (1957). This is over 100 lines long, rhyming inward from the first and last lines to reach a perfect contiguous couplet in the exact center. Since the distance tolerance of the mind for rhymes permits at best an intervening passage of, say, ten lines, Thomas has deliberately violated traditional rhyme schemes and ordinary linguistic capabilities. Over that distance no reader is willing to see if rhyme pairs are semantically like: certainly not the reader with Augustan tastes, whose tolerance for the spread of prosodic pattern rarely extends further than two lines.

EXPECTATION

Any account of poetry as a reiterative figure of sound must provide a sketch of how a reader's frustrated expectation may bring aesthetic pleasure. By what laws are the recurring sounds held apart? All verbal behavior uses two basic modes of arrangement, selection and combination. Selection of rhymes is based on lexical equivalences of similarity and dissimilarity (similar word endings, dissimilar word beginnings), and of synonymity and antonymity (same or opposite, or at least different, meaning of the rhyme words). The combination in rhyming poetry, the build up of the sequence (in Roman Jakobson's words), is based on the syntax, the coming-one-after-the-other of parts of the sentence. Typically and traditionally, the rhyming words, selected because homophones, are placed at line ends and mark off lines for the ear. In this way lexis and syntax are bound and overdetermined each by the other.[44]

As a device, then, rhyme has to do both with the selection and the placement of the words that chime. Equivalence of selection of the words themselves as entities is in fact taken further, into the construction of the discourse, by certain additional rules. These rules of meter usually create lines of equal lengths: syllables are "equalized" in meter, so that accented syllables receive more or less equal stress, unaccented receive more or less equal unstress. (Formal meter requires only that we register difference between stress and unstress, and remains a strategy of "more or less" despite the fairly recent invention of a four-level accent system for the description of the prosody of English speech.) Since the relation of rhyme to reason is of combination as well as selection—rhyme exerting an influence on the arrangement of the rest of the line—rhyme and meter interanimate each other whereever they are found together.

From the perspective of human cognition of poetic language, many types of poetic shape are valid as they delay and resolve the energies of attention. Though there is a range of complexity, the sophisticated rhymes are no more or less reasonable or literary than the others. No matter how palpably different they may be in degree of intricacy of pattern, the rudimentary writings will also be termed complex because the precondition of literary equivalence is complexity. Any writer of art sentences separates his language from ordinary language by a conscious patterning, literature's version of the frame surrounding the picture or the framing silence before and after the music. The attempt of writers after 1795 to snatch away this frame, and with it the concept of the device, is necessary, noble, and finally futile—except in the sense that this urge is the true motor of stylistic dynamism and innovation in the aesthetics of modernity.

It is now time to deal with examples that show how the sequence is built up by the permutation of positioned sounds, examples from less sophisticated writing which have implications for theory. Here I explore permutations over different distances without much concern for what has been called prominent or permissible in our manuals of usage. In all cases adduced, the figure of sound is recognizably a pattern, though not one which might dazzle a traditional prosodist.

Literariness becomes a kind of structural surplus by adding constraints and equivalences to ordinary language. Sometimes this poem-making process is a matter of rudimentary arrangement, segmentation, or transposition as in puns, spoonerisms, anagrams, or in one form of concrete poetry:

> Fowl
> Fred owl
> Fox
> Fred ox
> Fred
> Fred red
> Harp
> Hans Arp[45]

Watching the addition of three letters and a space to "fowl," seeing an implication of the noun drawn out of it, to attend Ernst Jandl's "Names" is to be present at the creation of rhyme. Then the name "Fred" itself undergoes permutation and breakdown; after the first set of terms is exhausted there is a lateral sliding to "Harp," and a new, smaller set is begun on the same principle. The achievement is minor yet nobody will say it is unrelated to the effect of rhyme. The interest, though, of traditional rhyme is permutation over a greater distance. In that considerable vacancy between *bouts rimés,* the poet is obliged to stuff or dilate middles. As to the reader: just when one has come through a stretch of language, one is again reminded, by the framing rhyme, that this is poetry. So long as the middles themselves were very definitely specified into a certain number and configuration of stressed and un-stressed syllables, the eighteenth century loved this reminder given by the overspecification of line ends. The post-Roman-tics, Mallarmé and Jandl, have afforded extraordinary in-stances where word position and wordplay shade into rhyme, but most poetry will not risk such extremes of deviation.

Certain folk poems elide or wither the "middles" between rhymes, but not quite so far as in the Jandl piece:

> I saw the ghostesses,
> Sitting on the postesses,
> Eating of their toastesses,
> And fighting with their fistesses.[46]

The anecdotal element is extended to provide an absurd pre-text for the comic rhymes that fill the second half of each line. We have here a poem—admittedly not a good poem—where the alogical pattern, in Wimsatt's terminology, is plainly con-stitutive. Apparently all poetic sorts get the proportion they require of sensory to logical resistance, and in this playful instance the sensory aspects dominate the other. Here are two verses from the Midlands:

> Tell-tale-tit,
> Your tongue shall be slit,
> And every dog in the town shall have a bit.
>
> He got out of the muxy,
> And fell into the pucksy.[47]

In the first, each line doubles the length of the preceding line, yet all are pent to the ear, equalized by the rhyme. No matter what the line length, the rhyme has to thump, for it is the rhyme that creates the line; rhyme that marks off lines for the ear and thus, in the absence of a quantitative prosody, helps build the text from the smallest unit to the whole utterance. The second of these is more interesting from the point of view of selection, not of combination, suggesting as it does that "minimal rhyme" is the basis and staple of the device: fraternal rhyme words on the same piece of grammar, as here, are more likely to be semantically related along the lines of word families.[48] The rhyme on "muxy" is related to old words for the disagreeable, "mixen," "midden," and "muck," while "pucksy" (similar in being either dialectal or invented) intensifies a progression of ideas from bad to worse by repeating the nasty joke of the sound with the slight change of *m* to plosive *p*. The logic is crude, a simple antithesis. Alexander Pope would never venture such low dialectal sounds; nevertheless, far more intricately worked, such logics are often the groundwork of the Popian couplet as well.

From the point of view of combination, that variable usually neglected, I shall now consider a common utterance that accompanies, sometimes actually effects, performances. Jump-rope rhymes are said in chorus by twirlers, watchers, and the skipper, one line to each swing of the rope, and the rhyme itself usually commands the performer to step out of the game. Here are two rhymes recorded a century ago in Warwickshire and Shropshire:

> Hickery, hoary, hairy Ann,
> Busybody, overspan,
> Pare, pare, virgin mare,
> Pit, pat, out, one.

> Ink, pink, pen and ink,
> I command you for to wink,
> Rottom, bottom, dish clout,
> O. U. T. spells out,
> So out goes she.[49]

The equivalences are within the line in rhyme or alliteration as well as from line to line (in "Pare, pare . . . / Pit, pat" successive lines open with two alliterating monosyllables). Yet only rarely, as in this from Northamptonshire, does this sort of utterance produce crossed rhymes instead of couplets:

> Hinks, spinks, and devil winks,
> The fat's beginning to fry,
> Nobody's home but Jumping Joan,
> Father, Mother, and I.
> O. U. T. out,
> With a long black snout,
> Out, pout, out.

Now, though "pout" orders (or describes) the feelings of the skipper who is out of the game, the content of these poems is usually nonsense. The poems may almost be said to exist for their rhymes, which in turn, in their emphatic position, direct the game and command exits from it.

The children who play are not aware of speaking in lines, and yet lines there are, measurable by the inflexible rule of the rope's swing. This rhyme numbers the lines out loud as it goes:

> Hickory (1),
> Dickory (2),
> Dock (3),
> The mouse ran up the clock (4),
> The clock struck one (5),
> The mouse was gone (6),
> O (7)
> U (8)
> T (9)
> Spells OUT!

Almost all folk rhymes and jumping rhymes are, as here, within limits eclectic in meter and line length. The lines are all equivalent in time length, as determined by the swinging rope; but sometimes the words are sung out slowly with pauses, sometimes they are hurried, words jammed. The letter "O" is here equal in time with "The mouse ran up the clock," the sort of equality-in-inequality which is most often

solidified by rhyme. The rhyme rescues the variant meters
too: encountering a saying that commands, "Butcher,
butcher, kill a calf," we expect a partner that is also perfectly
trochaic, but we get, "Hang him up, and eat half." The rhyme
naturalizes it.

There is a more meditative and literary kind of children's
poetry, where the child speaking as an individual (not as part
of a jump-rope chorus, with its communal invention and performance) comes to terms with what he or she knows of the
adult versification. This, by a seven-year-old American girl,
is called "My Private Life":

> In my private life, I think about things,
> Like I was a Queen with Diamond rings.
> And sometimes I think about trees and grass and flowers,
> And lots of princesses locked up in towers.
> And the only thing I like
> Is living in my private life.[50]

The first two couplets rhyme on nouns, "tame rhymes" in
Wimsatt's terms. But "like-life" in the final couplet is
remarkable, not only for the obliqueness of the sounds, one
to another, but especially because the rhyme uses "like" as a
verb, where at the beginning of the second line it is an
adverb—homoeoteleuton shading into rhyme, a logical shift
of no little subtlety. The title, when repeated as refrain in the
poem's first and last phrases, gives the effect of global wholeness and closure. The author knows the difference between a
masculine and a feminine rhyme, and though the lines are not
strictly equivalent in length, their differences—even the thir-
teen syllables of line three—do not seem obtrusive because of
the rhymes. Line lengths are apparently close enough; indeed
one might argue a certain flexibility for the line to extend or
contract as necessary according to the demands both of sense
and of allocating rhymes. The poem with the help of rhymes,
but not for their sake, involves thinking through beginning,
middle, end. One does not want to say that the sensuous
elements overwhelm the logical ones. Thus the child, having

read little or no poetry, but having heard it read, struggles to find sensible and acceptable types of equivalence in her acts of both selection and combination. It seems the passion for the principle of equivalence, for the poetic function in language, begins early in the history of the race and of the individual. One need not make especially strong claims for the resulting poetry from oral tradition or from children; such writing is perfect in its imperfection. Enough, here, to prize its hand-to-mouth rhyming as one mark of genuineness, and to note how the major poetry of nearly every age has reformed itself by inspecting the more direct usage of the basic devices to be found in the genres usually considered subliterary.

ALLOCATION

In most rhyming poetry the device serves to articulate the major structural units; the "figure of sound" enables the "build up of the sequence." In composition and in the reader's developing comprehension of the text, rhyme, sentence, and line are mutually determinative. Rhyme, in gestalt terms, is figure on the ground of the sentence and the line, but at the same time it is ground for other prosodic or grammatical devices. Looking backward from the rhyme to its chiming word or words, the device is figure. Looking ahead to the different rhyme that follows next, unspecified and yet in form predictable on the basis of established pattern, the very same end word is in the cognitive sense a ground. From its line-end position the device can be taken either forward or back.

Considered as figure on the ground of the sentence and line, rhyme draws attention to its own prominence. Geoffrey Hartman has studied the way the traditional device makes "poles" regress "to a line-end position . . . while the rest of the verse is inserted between these rhymed ends."[51] In poetry, he says, the "elision of middle terms and overspecification of end terms" collapses the chain or sequence of the sentence. However not all poetry has the usual pattern, and in the time before free verse "Milton's rejection of rhyme is related to Hopkins' freeing rhyme from its fixed terminal position and making the last first (in sound-shape, not merely line-place)." Even in that large body of traditional end-rhyme poetry—the corollary is crucial for Hartman—the strength of the end terms depends on our seeing or hearing the elided middle members of the chain. The poet will adjust the units of his lines, so as to arrive at the right time, metrically, syntactically, upon his rhyme sound. It means trimming, extending, attending to limits, thinking back from the end over the whole sequence, considering the device both as figure and ground. It is a commonplace worth testing that such "enabling restraints of formal bondage"[52] help evoke the rest of the poem, developing compressed statement and linguistic innovation. In this section I inquire whether overdetermination at line end produces other sorts of overdetermination throughout line, stanza, and poem.

To return rhyme to its place in sentence and line will mean assessing the shape and strength of the middle terms. Some mild protest is in order against Victor Shklovsky's extreme statement about "filling the distances between rhymes with free phonic spots."[53] He doubtless refers to the sense of randomness engendered by the clutter of words between the overleaping rhymes. The intervening words are free in the sense that they are exempt from the requirement to rhyme, and yet they are very much semantic-syntactic thralls unless the rhymes themselves are to be seen as detachable stubs or tags at line end. In fact, Mayakovsky seems right to speak of rhyme as the tightening nail, or even more strongly as the dynamite that explodes at the end of the line's fuse. Rhyme is a subeffect of poetic closure, and as such acts to resolve or reinforce other effects, metrical and syntactical, as the poem proceeds.

Linguists have devised a "depth hypothesis" to measure the amount of syntactical delay, or frustration, the ordinary auditor can withstand without losing the thread of the sentence.[54] Students of poetic devices may find this useful as they trace the distance back into line and stanza one has to go to find the syntactical justification for the word that rhymes. Within limits, it would appear that the further one has to go, the more fully justified the rhyme will seem. Such a method may be extended by correlating it with a notion of poetic register: the more meditative lyrical poems will usually push back the syntactical justification to the early part, even the first line, of a segment like a quatrain; while certain types of poems, such as comic verses, require less depth of syntactical regression in the justification of the rhyme. Here, the term "justify" may be understood in the compositor's sense as well as the logician's.

Poetry's figure of sound is recursive and involves a leading forward and back of recurring harmonies and significances. As the reader gets further into the sequence, more and more elements of the discourse become determined. The effects of chance are themselves diminished in the course of the utterance, as the types and limits of recurrence are settled. That, no doubt, is what Jiři Levý means when he says that the cause of rhyme's aesthetic effect is "unexpectedness of the specific sequences of sounds, based on a deviation from stochastic distribution."[55] The chances of rhyme, that is, create a jolt in the reader when recurrent sound and significance interfere with the linear buildup of the sequence. Levý defines the three elementary principles of form in the art sentence, of value because they apply both to sound and to sense in the poem and because they are phrased as binary oppositions. These three principles are continuity-discontinuity, regularity-irregularity, and "regularity or irregularity in the arrangement of unequal units, i.e. a higher or lower entropy of the series . . ."; so defined, the three principles permit us to correlate the physical level of the text with the semantic level.[56] The effective rhyme, defined in these terms, will confirm grammatical expectations, and yet, since homophony is impermissible in ordinary language, indeed indicates in that context a kind of derangement, will at the same time frustrate semantic expectations. Teasingly, the device suggests a semantic link between words. Beyond the type of "reasonable rhymes" Wimsatt and others have discussed, this link can very likely never be proved, nor need it be.[57] What counts is the way the device in its place will both confirm and unsettle expectations. Pushkin and his translator Walter Arndt, for example, know just what the reader likes and have their fun with him:

> At last a crackling frost enfolded
> Fields silvered o'er with early snows
> (Alright—who am I to withhold it,
> The rhyme you knew was coming—ROSE!)[58]

The expected rhyme is given, despite its nonsense in context, and the poet shocks the reader out of his habitual associations of contrast, depriving him of the snows-rose cliché forever.

In admirable rhymed poems, there is a very high degree of unexpectedness in the intermittent shock when we discover a discourse, which seems natural, is in fact overdetermined by a line of devices of equivalence. How does the professional poet deploy these equivalences, hiding the labor as he crafts the line up to the rhyme, back from the rhyme? Consider the syntactical regression back from the final line in Robert Graves:

> Impossible men: idle, illiterate,
>   Self-pitying, dirty, sly,
> For whose appearance even in City parks
>   Excuses must be made to casual passers-by.[59]

This workmanlike stanza takes one risk, the placement of "sly" at line end, precarious after the comma. This is justified by the submergence of vocalic effects (*i* sounds in lines 1–2), the dropping of rhymes off the ends of lines 1 and 3, and by the way "passers-by" almost diffidently picks up the rhyme. Lines 3–4 are built of a long appositional phrase, equal to "sly" in adding one last piece of information to the list of ad-

jectives, yet unequal in length. The syntactical justification
for the rhyme word goes back at least to "For"—but eventually, I believe, to the colon in the first line with the poten-
tiality implied there for the list that follows. If the example is
accepted as typical, we must substitute for Shklovsky's "free
phonic spots" another description by Juri Tynjanov, who
speaks of "the crowdedness of the poetic lines." The poet may
achieve this compression of meanings by sheer stretch of
naked grammar, but more often will employ a phrasal sentencing, with apposition, clots of phrase, stops and starts.
Most poets, rhyming in fairly short bursts, partition the line
and poem into smaller subsets by caesura, juncture, and various effects of breaking off.

I have been arguing that sound and sense in literary composition determine each other reciprocally, no place more evidently than in rhyming practice. I have tried to show this, up
to now, by using examples from fairly simple verse forms.
Before further examples, and in order to schematize the
theory of allocation developed thus far, I would like to consider the case of Chinese poetry.[60] My attempt here, too, is to
try to slow down and space out the analysis of the composition process.

Chinese, because it is morphematic and not alphabetic,
partitions the line by ideograms and not words, gaining thus a
more clipped rhythm than Western languages. Its very difference from the English manner of proceeding makes it valuable
as a theoretical model for allocation. The use of end rhyme is
exactly the same as in English, but the system of constraints is
otherwise revealingly different. One highly common form of
the eight-line-regulated poem contains, in each line, five ideograms; each of these is either deflected or level in tone. The
rule is that deflected-tone and level-tone ideograms must
alternate along the line. If this first line is to rhyme (with lines
2, 4, 6, and 8), it must end on a level-tone ideogram. Then,
working back from the rhyme position, ideograms 2, 3, and 4

in the line are strictly determined while the first remains optional and may be either deflected or level. The model of Chinese shows, in a clearer way than in English, that the line as an entity progresses from indeterminacy to determinacy. This holds true of the presumed act of composition and also in the reader's version of that act when the line is taken in perceptually. If the line is to rhyme, the whole thing is determined all the way back to the second ideogram; only the first ideogram may be taken with any freedom between the two choices, and even then we have a normal mode and a variant. The Chinese poetic line is a string of binary oppositions: once the decision to rhyme is made for the first line of the poem, a whole series of other constraint operations comes into play. To choose to rhyme shuts off other options, while the choice not to rhyme provides slightly more free option in line 1. As one gets further into line or into sentence or poem, constraints increase in quantity and determining power.

Apparently Chinese, with its rhythms and excitements different from ours, cannot achieve the special expectation of syntactical delay or the pleasurable frustration of the English periodic sentence. With ideograms as equal units, juncture and disjuncture are insistent, but Chinese will not display the specific track of feeling of the Western languages, which do not so strongly employ separation of the parts of the line. There are in English, that is, more units (words) in a given line; therefore more partitions; and therefore the line is more possessed of continuity. The more you partition down, the more continuity you achieve. What results from this process may, however, be a spurious or rhapsodic continuity, of the sort one finds sometimes in a writer like Swinburne. Thus when, as with Pound, a writer wanted the laconicism of the clumped phrase, he consciously imitated, in English, the Chinese mode.

Meaning and organization are processes that occur in a medium and depend on that medium's properties. The linear character of writing obliges us to measure, if only subjectively in ourselves as readers, what information theorists call the channel capacity of the receiver. The spans of immediate and long-term memory impose severe limits on the amount of information we are able to receive and remember. As readers, we will have psycholinguistic limits, historically and personally determined, upon our matching responses to a given writer's strings of language. One writer on the psychology of communication has argued that human memory can span seven items, plus or minus two.[61] Without declaring what such an "item" might be in prosody, but rather remembering length of lines or of distance between rhymes in traditional poetry, we can at least say that poetry in all languages will develop a line neither too long nor too short for the active memory to find its proper play. Except in poems of the extreme avant-garde, lines have enough "crowdedness" of equivalence to keep continuous interest, but they do not extend the pattern-response capacity very far beyond normal endurance. Rhymes will seem bolder in short-line poems, because, in Geoffrey Hartman's term, there is less middle to be "elided." But in lines of any length, the compositional value of rhyme will be its ability to introduce a cross pattern against the system of stresses: rhyme must, as Henry Lanz says, "be something apart from rhythm in order to assist us rhythmically."[62] Since counting stressed syllables is not a habit of natural language reception, we require as line marker a type of equivalence which does not get heard because it is rhythmically prominent, but because it is melodically pleasing. Thus in traditional poems, the actual unit of construction becomes the rhyme-linked pair, broader in its sweep than the single line of verse. Free verse, deprived of such a sweep of pattern, can, if it wants, give the line and its parts a more distinct integrity than traditional verse. Then again, as Jan M. Meijer has affirmed, some structural principles are dynamic forces. Once set in motion, meter and rhyme can go on and on: "It is a structural principle other than rhyme that puts an end to the process."[63] Meter wants rhyme to demarcate line ends, while rhyme craves some principle of substantive plot to halt the poem. The aesthetic structure absolutely requires the cognitive structure in order to realize itself: medium depends on meaning.

A highly developed constraint system can be shown to operate in texts whose form is prescribed, and whose very vocabulary is determined by arbitrary rule before the poem begins. In *New Stateman* Weekend Competition No. 2,213, "competitors were asked to compose a Shakespearean sonnet containing the following words or phrases: gentian, charisma, cradle, burgeon, *cri de coeur*, investment, helpless, alopecia, run of the mill, allocate, devices, runcorn."[64] So length and number of lines, as well as disposition of rhymes into one kind of sonnet, is fixed. Roughly one-quarter of the poem's language is already specified: seventeen words in all, none rhyming. The best two solutions were:

> When Runcorn's gentians first refused to burgeon
> And what divided it from fuming Widnes
> Flowed thick with chemicals instead of sturgeon,
> Helpless to filter as nephritic kidneys,
> Only some dotty poets really got
> The sense of England's coming alopecia—
> Trees allocated to the villa's plot,
> To little rooms of glass and vine and freesia.
> Most others, swayed by the charisma of
> Investment, simply raised their *cri de coeur*
> For the still freer run of the mill. Their love
> Of cash and devices made whole skies a blur.
> Cradle of ugliness and muck, the North:
> Why do I cherish all that you put forth?
>
> Pope mocked Belinda on whose helpless nape
> Her lover bold, despite the sylph's devices,
> Committed with his scissors such foul rape
> As should be starred with Coma Berenicis.

I sing a Runcorn Lady of the Game
Her charms her sole investment. Gentian eyes
Lured lovers; her charisma called; some came,
Run of the mill types; she'd been no great prize

From cradle days. But, when hair ceased to burgeon,
She allocated cash from funds not big
To have her *cri de coeur* heard by a surgeon.
Bald patches? Alopecia! Buy a wig.

So should Belinda, shorn of crowning glory
Have born a Whig, not suffered Pope, a Tory.

In the first sonnet the octet is a single sentence. This sentence
is a series of right-branching, or dependent, clauses. Every
sentence unit is a subdivision of the next-higher unit. The
length and complexity of the sentence is gained by embedding
of clauses. In turn, this embedding is related to, perhaps
caused by, the constraint introduced by the rhymes.[65]
Embedding of clauses is one of the phenomena of the intruded
middle; the clauses fall like continual parentheses of thought,
a recoil of the sentence upon itself to catch a detail or nuance
before progressing forward.

We are either, it seems, running with the eyes and mind up
to the rhymes, or away from them along the next line.
Rhymes exert attraction toward themselves, then once past,
repulsion; or propulsion along the ensuing line toward the
next rhyme. I am describing the reader's experience of that elision of middles which interests other disciplines than literature.[66] The couplet is the most memorable rhyme form,
because of its maximal closure and its more regular arrangement of words as units of unequal length. Eighteenth-century
rhyming tried with the strict couplet to revise all devices by
multiplying, so far as possible, the elements of predictability.
One difference between Pope and writers since 1795 lies in
post-Romanticism's enormously expanded tolerance for
effects of chance and the reader's frustration.

One of the less convincing solutions to the *New Statesman* task has this ending:

> How can this metre—tell me, if you will—
> Accommodate the phrase "run *of* the mill"?

A good trick to perform what one claims is impossible, and that, in the act of claiming: it is of genuine metrical interest that the "of" in the last line gets emphasis by position and italics, and achieves the curious effect of seeming stressed and scudded at once. And yet the rhyme on "if you will" seems stitched onto the end of the line. Apparently rhymes are seamless only when the syntax leading up to them does not include effects of apposition or of parataxis or of interpolated parenthesis. The further back in the line or stanza one can trace the syntactic justification for the rhyme word, the easier it will be to afford the necessary slight shock of the unfamiliar. Here, as in the example from Robert Graves, the chances of rhyme involve our continually encountering in discourse the improbable effects of equivalence at regular or fairly regular intervals. These effects signal the aesthetic function.

By rhyming French or Latin terms with English ones, the two sonnets quoted in full create even more dissimilarity than in the case of mere grammatical unlikes; so the effect is still wittier ("coeur-blur"; "devices-Berenicis"). Other types of equivalence reinforce meanings in these sonnets:

Only some dotty poets really got
  (internal rhyme)

The still freer run of the mill
  (internal rhyme; imitative phrasing in "run of the mill," which skips a stress and suggests by prosody that freer attitude)

Bald patches? Alopecia! Buy a wig.
  (trisected line; representation of dialogue; exaggerated juncture suggesting symptom, diagnosis, and treatment compressed into one line)

Have born a Whig, not suffered Pope, a Tory.
    (parallel or antithetical syntax; pun on Whig-wig; internal rhyme
    with "shorn" in previous line)

It might be said that in "Pope mocked Belinda," the rhyme on
"not big" is awkward, because the final phrase inverts normal
order of adjective and noun; but I think this is, like "lover
bold" in line 2, a conscious oddity, deliberately prominent. It
is the kind of phrase which trains irony on the subject in order
to diminish it. In addition to meeting all the requirements of
the competition, both poems have a very high density of
various sorts of equivalence. For the sake of incongruity, I
compare lines from a more relaxed convention that gets its
effects not from connection but from disjunction, not from
syntax but from juxtaposed catalogs. The equivalences here
are those of simple antithesis, and the lines, from Thomas
Hood, perhaps provide a very rough English equivalent to the
Chinese manner of proceeding:

> Now double entry—now a flowery trope—
> Mingling poetic honey with trade wax—
> Blogg, brothers—Milton—Grote and Prescott—Pope—
> Bristles—and Hogg—Glyn Mills and Halifax—
> Rogers—and Towgood—Hemp—The Bard of Hope—
> Barilla—Byron—Tallow—Burns—and Flax![67]

The superimposition of two different and conflicting systems
of rhyme and meaning gives to these last lines the effect of a
Petrarchan sonnet: the contrast of ideal and trivial. Rhymes
seem blundered upon, though of course they are carefully
planned. There is no nuance or quantity of information which
must be comprised in these lines at all comparable to the density or flow of the other sonnets. The tone of the catalog is
desired, and what usually seems a defect—rhyme's very facti-
tiousness—is here turned to a stylistic preference.

Under the conditions of the competition, successful poems
were bound to come up with a density of style. The proportion of aesthetic information to the available containers is

high, of an extreme near to the situation taken to hyperbole by Anthony Burgess in his commentary on last-minute touches to his lyrics for the Broadway musical, *Cyrano*:

Telephone calls come through demanding fiddling modifications to lyrics. To an unchangeable musical rhythm, in twenty-four syllables, in two lines rhyming—ound, the following information must be imparted to the audience: It is fourteen years since my lover was killed in battle, and since that time I have been living in this convent, seeing the beloved as both dead and living at the same time, somehow a god of the season, but not really dead in the winter and resurgent in the spring, instead possessed of the winter's constancy, not grimness, as well as the loving liveliness of nature in the spring and summer, and clothed in the magnificence of autumn.[68]

Perhaps because the two sonnets quoted are very special instances of highly overspecified relationships of end to middle, more than other rhyming poems they raise the question whether external constraints in themselves produce aesthetic density. In both sonnets, intruded middles have been strengthened, either to offset or to justify four features or restraints—the overspecified ends, the prescribed diction, the sonnet form, and the iambic ground pattern. It is hard to deny that in these examples there is a causal connection between formal limitation and multiplicity of poetic equivalences. Yet not all equivalences are of this highly specified nature. More random conventions of weakened conventional shape do exist, and from these emerge equivalences, which, though hard to recognize as such because of the obscuring of overt pattern, are equally valid. Modern poetry takes as its project the systematic blurring or dilution of the inherited constraints, and its poetics requires a description of the shapes that result, shapes weakened in the cognitive but not necessarily in the aesthetic sense.

FAILURE

The seasoned poet's task of allocating all the parts of the line is not essentially different in kind from the failed poet's. The linguistic and cognitive differentials between literary poetry and inferior or nonliterary poetry are rather small. Slight differentials in quantity and placement make major differences in aesthetic valuation. This makes it hard to define the distinctive nature of literariness.

Yet the poetic devices, and the labor they imply, do seem highly obtrusive in the failed poem. When the egregious rhyme leaps out at us from the awful poem, we suddenly see how the meaning of this and all devices

lies in their relation to a structural whole of interrelated meanings and intentions. In breakdown, for a brief moment the meaning of the objects is lighted up, emerging directly. . . . A broken hammer at once shows what a hammer is.[69]

If we conceive the poem, any poem, as a fabric worked up from the mutual interference of an aesthetic and a cognitive principle, it will follow that we should see each of these two principles trying to reduce the other to matter. To the extent that the aesthetic and the cognitive have not achieved a balance of forces, the not-fully-achieved work is a lump of words.[70] As it happens the bad poet who rhymes is usually bad in a certain way. In the examples that follow, perhaps in all examples of failed rhyming, the cognitive principle is overpowering and reduces the aesthetic to language matter. The flagrant rhyme draws attention to its overdetermination. In the most laughable instances, one can always tell which of two rhyming words the poet who fails hit upon first.

Robert Lowell, like all translators of poetry, admits to a final inadequacy. All translation is failure in the sense that, as Lowell has said, sound effects are not

transferrable from one language to another. I know what Baudelaire's sound effects are like and I try to get something else in English. . . . The Baudelaire was very hard for me, just to rhyme. I first did them in blank verse, then tried to rhyme them. I really did countless versions, shifting, changing lines.[71]

Those blank-verse versions were matrices, draft stages. It seems a particularly delicate stage, if one has decided that the rhymes must be preserved. Rhyme must be justified structurally, not only back into the syntax of the line and stanza but also by reference to the exact level of diction in the original. Similarly in Walter Arndt's Pushkin, the *Eugene Onegin* stanza has an "ordered interplay of masculine and feminine rhymes, and three differently patterned iambic tetrameter quatrains with a couplet at the end."[72] Arndt speaks of his work of rearrangement and omission: "Predictably, most occur at the end of lines." We are reminded by this that rhyme is a prominent effect; perhaps more than the meter itself, rhyme influences the character of the entire utterance. Arndt believes Vladimir Nabokov's *Onegin* translation, which omits the rhymes, fails to do justice to the original. The literal line-for-a-line method, he argues, is a form of naive realism about the nature of literary style:

Poetic utterance is not produced from some underlying, neutral, merely cognitive statement by linguistic manipulation; and if it were the manipulations could not be the same in language A as in language B, or else they would be the *same* language. Hence sequential literalness becomes worse than irrelevant.

One would have to show, as I cannot, that Arndt gives more of Pushkin than Nabokov. Clearly Nabokov's version is premised upon a fine disdain, a belief that the sound effects are not to be captured, so not worth botching; whereas Arndt, like Lowell, believes the translator represents, not reproduces rhyme in the original.

Though all translators fail, nonetheless the adequate ones are always in the first instance adept readers of texts in their native languages. This permits them to see that, as Arndt says,

the proper formal frame of accuracy, i.e. the largest allowable unit of form within which maximum fidelity must be achieved, is a delicate matter of balancing the poetic pulse of the original against the stylistic sense of the reader in the target language, and against his syntactic comprehension span.

Despite the success, though, of Arndt's modest Pushkin in rhymes and of Lowell's splendid Baudelaire, many translators —having held all the factors in balance—have decided that for certain poems rhyme will not come across. They omit some or all of the sound effects, and concentrate on presenting a poem's line of images and emotional logic. Some such decision was made by the French translator of Robert Lowell and John Berryman, Alain Bosquet, who gives the last couplet of Lowell's "To Speak of Woe That is in Marriage,"

> Gored by the climacteric of his want
> He stalls above me like an elephant,

as

> Aguillonné par le retour de ses besoins,
> Il s'empetre au-dessus de moi comme un éléphant.[73]

Lowell's rhyme is imperfect, ferocious. Missing it, the French gives the inherently weak simile of the last line far more force than it has in Lowell's English. What is aggressively ugly in the original is carried, to a large extent, by the deformed rhymes.

John Berryman's "Note to Wang Wei" finds rhymes for every line, but M. Bosquet has been able to pair only half the poem's lines:

> How could you be so happy, now some thousand years
> Disheveled, puffs of dust?
> It leaves me uneasy at last,
> your poems tease me to the verge of tears
> and your fate. It makes me think.
> It makes me long for mountains & blue waters.
> (I'm reconfirming, God of bolts & bangs,
> of fugues & bucks, whose rocket burns & sings.)
> I wish we could meet for a drink
> in a 'freedom from ten thousand matters.'
> Be dust myself pretty soon; not now.

> Comment peux-tu être si heureux, défait depuis
> quelque mille ans, boufées de poussière?

> J'en éprouve un malaise à la fin:
> tes poèmes me taquinent jusqu'au bord des larmes
> comme ton destin. Cela me fait songer.
> Cela me fait désirer montaignes & eaux bleues.
> Me fait désirer quot permettre.
> (Je me rassure, Dieu de tonnerres & d'éclairs,
> de fugues & de béliers, dont la fusée brûle & chante.)
> J'aurais aimé que nous nous rencontrions pour un verre
> dans un 'délivrance des dix mille matières'.
> Serai poussière moi-même bientôt; pas maintenant.

In the French, lines 1 and 3–7 are unrhymed, and it takes till line 8 for "poussière" to find its mate. Bosquet rhymes the last line with the ninth, but in Berryman it rhymes further back (line 7), producing a closer interweaving of end sounds in the final two-thirds of the original. Berryman's "not now" might seem spliced on the end of the last line, unjustifiably; but he wants clipped, pitiless tones here: cutting out personal pronouns and working with sentence torsos, he manages without a hint of self-pity to deal with his own mortality and need for fame. "Now" is rhymed back into the body of the poem (twice, on "how" and "allow" in line 7), so as not to appear obtrusive; partly hidden by distance, the rhyme is implicative. The French goes some way toward managing this terseness, yet ends with the diffused register of the long word, "maintenant." Unpredictably but always firmly, Berryman's rhyme binds the whole and keeps the parts separated. Rhyme in the French version does not, to the same extent, convey a tone by sound, meaning, and placement.

Translations, though, are rarely perfect failures. No inadequate translator will ever, like the immortal William McGonagall, be admired and reprinted for transcendent badness:

> 'Twas in the year of 1869, and on the 19th of November
> Which the people in Southern Germany will long remember,
> The great rain-storm which for twenty hours did pour down,
> That the rivers were overflowed and petty streams all around.[74]

The lines are stuffed full of grammatical (and ungrammatical) odd lots and lengths in order to make up the approximate weight to balance them. Words are cut ("'Twas") or phrases spun out ("did pour down"), clauses are connected by an unnecessary "which" or "that," or by running "ands" of parataxis: all in order to make the middles of lines roughly equal. The same is true of the meter, which without transition is either mechanic doggerel or utterly irregular. Thus does sublime inferior verse hang its lines on hooks of rhyme. Like folk poets and children, many bad poets believe that to have poetry, one must have rhyme. Here are the first two of twenty-five stanzas that were found framed on a landlady's wall in Pacific Beach, California. The author has McGonagall's anxious need to pin down date and place at the start:

> It was on October thirty-first, nineteen hundred and thirty-one
> That, the family and friends at the N—— home had such great fun!
> I feel moved to write about it, and let Mrs. N—— know
> How glad I am, that I was invited to R——'s wedding to go.
>
> When I first heard that R—— was to be married some weeks ago
> I thought, oh, that's far distant. But how quickly time goes. So
> Now it is in the past. The event was last Saturday night,
> That Dr. M—— tied the not, and I'm sure he did it right.[75]

The need to rhyme devalues the middles of the poem, all the parts inside the rhymes. The predominance of the cognitive over the aesthetic principle, in Meijer's terms, skews any right relation of rhyme to the rest of the line; so one lurches from rhyme to rhyme, foothold to desperate foothold over fifteen or sixteen syllables. With the drastic extension of middles, all must be spelled out, embellished. With its dead metaphors and inversions, its oddity of juncture ("goes. So / "), its grasping for clichés to make the rhyme, and the rhyme conceived as makeweight of any clutter so as to get out to the right-hand end, the poem is a disaster. It is thereby unintentionally charming. One feels in the presence of the thing itself.

Many of the received rules for making up lines or for rhyming are here violated with the impunity of ignorance. Yet rule violation, whether deliberate or unconscious, is never a mistake in principle. What happens here is but a glorious extension of effects present in all good rhymed and metered verse. Only when poems like these, which succeed as formalized communications to special audiences, are brought near professional poetry for comparison, will the question of judgment arise and the rhymes seem, as Stevens would say, unpardonably expected. The special audience of such a poem would have a sense of poetic form, and of the limits and possibilities of the occasion, so withered and restricted as to permit such writing to have meaning and great value for them. They see the trouble the writer took on their behalf, the labor to produce such an evidently rule-bound object. The marks of labor and of duty are all over the poem that is traditional—and bad!

Awful poems have a terrible force of seriousness and concern. The urgency of the cognitive principle, the need to communicate, apparently short-circuits aesthetic premeditation. Two final instances:

> Other days and other names come to mind with ease:
> Nathan Hale, Lincoln, Wilson of the League;
> And now he too is gone as well as these,
> All felled by irony and hate's intrigue.
> Yet now his words and spirit are made free
> The newest witness to our liberty.

> You're the dream in my heart
> That's dearer to me
> Than the air I breathe—
> Barry Blue.

> You're the singer I love
> My dear turtle dove . . .
> Oh, if I could be true
> To this star who's so new—

> Barry Blue . . .
> I'd be over the moon with you![76]

The between-rhyme middles are devalued metrically, syntactically, in register shifts, inability to count, failures of euphony; while the unsubtle ends of lines positively shout their rhymes. The content has here rendered as malleable material the structure of the line; rhyme never had a chance. And these passages have the advantage of a more or less traditional scaffolding; ineffectual free verse is perhaps in even greater danger of building up a surfeit of like sounds that do not justify their positions, thus freeing but not renewing rhyme.

INNOVATION

Some tasks of construction, rhyme cannot perform; others, the unpardonably expected, it has performed only too well. With few exceptions modern poets decide to keep the device of rhyme but warp and reposition it. The need to reinvent the device from within has produced original types and placements for the ancient method of sound linkage. At no other time since the Middle Ages, when rhyme in English verse was an exotic foreign import, has the device been pulled and squeezed so experimentally. Most poets after 1910 are represented by Marianne Moore's statement: "Concealed rhyme and the interiorized climax usually please me better than the open rhyme and the insisted-on climax."[77] In the work of many major poets this preference has resulted in a drastic weakening of shape; not the abandonment of form, but an increased unpredictability of rhyming effects that must afford another, not necessarily a keener, pleasure to the reader.

One way of arranging the modern examples in this section would be to set them out according to degrees of distortion and avoidance of the traditional line-end position. To this account could be added a survey of types and intensities of modern deviations of rhyme sounds from "perfect" rhyme, from a construct that could be educed from the sound values of traditional rhyming between Chaucer and Tennyson. Instead I have chosen a literary schema that moves from sound play in rhyme to sense play in rhyme. The sequence of the following passages will put conventional rhyming behavior near the midpoint of a spectrum between two extremes of language pathology, beginning with nonsense or echolalia and ending with multiple sense or punning. More than any previous period's work, modern rhyme exemplifies all points on the range, including the extremes. So these examples suggest that the same modernity that officially denies the device may also, if with some violence, find its renewal indispensable.

It is easy to pass over lines like:

> Co co rico co co rico

or

> Drip drop drip drop drop drop drop

in Eliot's *Waste Land*, yet the bits of rhyming nonsense disorient the reader, suggesting the flashing-up of a hallucinative state:

> Weialala leia
> Wallala leialala.

The ending of Hugh MacDiarmid's "In the Slums of Glasgow" also stretches internal rhyme to the limit, almost completely obliterating meaning in the technical sense of the term; but the effect of being no longer, or not yet, rhyme, is exactly chosen as the final movement of a long meditation on poverty:

Now the babel of Glasgow dies away in our ears,
The great heart of Glasgow is sinking to rest,
Na nonanunno nunno nana nananana nanu,
Nunno nunnonanunneno nanena nunnannunanut.
We lie cheek to cheek in a quiet trance, the moon itself no more still.
There is no movement but your eyelashes fluttering against me,
And the fading sound of the work-a-day world,
Dadadoduddadadadaddadi dadadodudadidadoh.
Duddadam dadade dudde dadadadaddodododah.[78]

Eliot and MacDiarmid are not the first to mute the significa-cation of words and to exaggerate the seeming autonomy of the system of sounds. In this mode Velimir Khlebnikov and Edith Sitwell were, among others, early experimenters. And Wallace Stevens, after his embarrassment at the overt rhyming in his "June Book," went on to weave into a lengthy blank verse poem the multiple sound values of the letter C. "You have to think of this incidentally as you read ["The Comedian as the Letter C"]," Stevens said in a letter, "You cannot think of it directly. . . . You have to read the poem and hear all this whistling and mocking and stressing and, in a minor way, orchestrating, going on in the background or, to say it as a lawyer might say it, 'in, on or about the words.'"[79] Stevens is overmodest; the effect is not so noticeable as rhyme; yet neither is it minor. The "stressing" in this poem was implicated enough with essential meaning for him to draw attention to it in the title. In Stevens, and notably in Khlebnikov and Apollinaire, such effects are sometimes wrongly praised as "sensitivity to pure sound."[80] So far as an aesthetic intention is evident, the sound is not "pure" but has value in and by its slight semantic residue. However, to the extent that any poet piles up sound effects his poem will seem to evade semantic logic, and the whistling and mocking of his quasi rhymes may appear the quintessence of imaginative play. Rhyme is such cases is always conscious challenge to ordinary language: flamboyant surplusage of sound pattern which—even in the word games of concrete poetry—never quite eludes the control of a discoverable, commonsense logic.

Encountering Steven's "Commedian as the Letter C" for the first time, one may not realize that a local consonance was part of a vast intentional orchestration. Here as elsewhere in recent writing the relation between instance and design is masked and appears unsystematic. For some purposes, for some poets, the line-end position is untouchable now, and the device migrates into the line. W. H. Auden in "Pleasure Island" uses internal rhymes on the penultimate vowel, thus:

> What there is as a surround to our figures
>   Is very old, very big,
> Very formidible indeed; the ocean
>   Stares right past us as though
> No one here was worth drowning. . . .[81]

Kenneth Rexroth loads rhymes into the second section of "Andromeda":

> Anguish and form and prayer
> No excuse no betrayal
> No dimension in space or time
> Without caution without consequence without motion
> The many blades of the revolving razors
> The many tears of the breaking sorrow
> The fear of the bear the ghost of the bear
> The gear of care that is always here
> When the cross of words spells zero
> There are threes in the sea
> There are red columns on the horizon
> And fear everywhere
> And every year no word at all for her pain[82]

That sort of thing can go on endlessly, and yet Rexroth knows how to terminate one sequence and begin another, alternating tones and contexts as well as rhyme sounds, rhyme places. In the final lines of Norman Nicholson's "The Black Guillemot," line-end rhyme is only part of the clustering of equivalences:

> But, turn the page of the weather,
> Let the moon hand up the tides and the pressure-hose of spray
> Swill down the lighthouse lantern—Then,
> When boats keep warm in harbour and bird-watchers in bed,
> When the tumble-home of the North Head's rusty hull
> Takes the full heave of the storm,
> The hundred white and the one black flock
> Back to the same rock.[83]

In every way this sounds an ending, with four *ck* words out of the last seven. The resource is the more powerful for being spared for definite effects.

Another sort of writing, neither primitive nor traditional, uses and overrides rhymes within the line and at line end. These verses are chanted to a drum by "The Last Poets," a group of militant Blacks who have original priorities as to what must be carved away from the device to keep it vivid. I take these lines from the album notes of a record:

> Selfish desires are burning like fires among those
> who horde the gold
> As they continue to keep the people asleep and the
> truth from being told
> Racism and greed keep the people in need from getting
> what's rightfully theirs
> Cheating, Stealing and Double Dealing as they exploit
> the people's fears.
> Now Dow Jones owns the people's homes and all
> the surrounding land,
> buying and selling their humble dwelling in the name
> of the master plan
> 'Cause paper money is like a bee without honey with
> no stinger to back him up,
> And those who stole the people's gold are definitely
> corrupt. . . .[84]

We will not find some of these rhymes in any rhyming dictionary. These lines are also aggressively destructive of formal meter. Yet this voice has its own measures and insistent tones; it would take a hearing of the record itself to bear out a claim I should like to make, namely that in this instance poem-as-heard is superior to poem-as-read. What appears here on the page is a set of notations for a voice that can ignore the conventions of meter. In this voice there is not the kind of wit one finds in twentieth-century Popian verse, and yet there is wit,

logical progression, speed. The poem savors the rhymes but
drives beyond, ticking them off:

> Now the U.S. mints on paper prints, millions every day
> and use the
> Eagle for their symbol, 'cause its a bird of prey.

Since this is to be taken in by the ear, in print it seems thrown
onto the page. Yet there is nothing loose or unjustified. There
are three stresses in each long line, resounding and lingering
stresses only on the rhymes. Read with these stresses, the lines
sort themselves out and convey their own decorum.

One might illustrate other possibilities with a poem whose
rhyming segments have not been surpassed in subtlety in this
century, Eliot's "Ash Wednesday"; or by such a splendid
piece of chance-seeming rhyme as Robert Lowell's "Man and
Wife." But instead, for something yet more difficult to explain
by the more usual analytical tools, here are two passages
from Edward Dorn's *Slinger*:

> From a point on the arc
> 2 days minus 2 corners
> We sure know where that's at Boss, um
> We can find it *in the Dark*
>
> O Poet, Hey Poet! the sun like a sword
> Cuts below the Tanner's Yard
> and we must hear the effect formed
> of the code name Rupert another time
> Another time we will witness
> how this double hydrocarbon hustles the future
> but for now, *Later on*
> Fresh Distortions have swept the screen
> And from the smell brought in by the wind
> we have news of the Master Nark
> who trailed us into your cycle
> Yet there is another, an *Unknown*
> who tracks us
> Someone whose *fame* is his Name
> A summer storm advances Though it is autumn
> You will conclude in another Town

Away from the shades
When under the cool strokes of *Muthos*
we'll find out about
which way that Epactos goes

For some while we parallel the train
whose shining rails are closed at both horizons
and this group in which our brain
is contained, speaks in the excellent tones
of the beginning of an ascent, feel them rising
into the realm of the surprising
bent over what they say
along the river Rio Grande
'earing the low chordes of the foothills
spitting the seeds of the Sandias
out of the corners of their eyes
as they rise
towards the land of the crazy Utes
over and thru the mordants
of the bridges and the buttes[85]

Rhymes fall at line ends but not always or predictably. There is a wish to rhyme, but not to take the whole thing too seriously as a formal scheme. A line might just as easily end with "um." In the first passage, the end of a major part of the long poem, there is a massing of peculiar consonant chimes as a signal of closure ("sword-yard," "formed-time," "on-screen," rhymes like Wilfred Owen's pararhymes). The second passage is more systematic, but here too line length and the closeness of rhyme words in sound move within highly variable limits, so one is never fully sure a rhyme has been encountered. We have, too, the curious though not isolated case of rhymed lines that are by intention unmetered. These lines parade their artifice: their carefully disarranged measures open to the reader's regard the allocational tasks of the rhyming poet. The lines do not claim to be anything other than slightly jerry-built, and the humor in this is related to the humor of a mixed diction where, in the space of twenty lines,

"Nark" and "Muthos" and "hydrocarbon" can extend each others' frame of reference. With such conventions this writing is a laughing allusion to the resources and deficiencies of a reigning prosody. The poet has learned enough of that prosody to send it up, though here as everywhere, he will keep more elements than he wants to throw away.

A major theorist of rhyme, Viktor Zhirmunski, speaks of it as a secondary factor in composition, "a means of uniting the rhythmical line into a structural unit of a higher order (the stanza)."[86] Zhirmunski's theory takes account of Mayakovsky's assertion that in this century secondary elements will usurp the primary place of meter itself; but he denies that there can be rhyme or rhythm without explicit, traditional scansion. He reaffirms the primacy of meter, independently in agreement with T. S. Eliot that there is no escape from meter, "only mastery." To contradict this I have already quoted measured but unmetered rhyming passages and more could be cited from such as Mayakovsky, Olson, Dorn, Robert Duncan, or, as here, from John Logan:

> The fog
>   stammers everywhere
> along the rock
>   break-
> water pier
>   and in the twilight air
> the Peace
> Bridge has its Buffalo steel feet
> nearly all cut off.
>   Therefore it walks
> like a lame centipede quite
> impotent at first
> then on to Canada.
> Fishermen
>   are chattering in
> the fog.
>   It's not
> just the sign of them on the shore
> I hear

but also the live laughter
of those boys with their poles
moving toward us,
breaking through the holes in the mist
which again will fill.[87]

Intended or not, in speech or in poetry, meter is always present. Metrical categories are always precise, or at any rate aim at precision. It would be possible to attempt scansion of this or the Dorn passages, but would it be appropriate? Would metrical analysis help us to describe the key patterns of these poems where meter was so obviously not intended? It seems to me that the central pattern of Logan's lines is rather a figure of sound wherein words are keyed to one or more other words somewhere within the range of aural memory. Of many patterns, one: "pier" reaches above to "everywhere"; below to "air," "nearly," and both halves of "therefore." All these words are given emphasis by line break and juncture, and their placement gives energy to nearly every possible place in the line. This visual isolation of keyed sounds, combined with visual and aural continuities forward and back, makes the passage at once eventful and casual, reducing the prominence of the rhymes while at the same time catching each rhyme firmly. A pattern emerges and a tone is managed, though without the help of an abstract metrical scheme.

No other poet could employ these measures of Logan's, unless he repeated exactly the same poem. And yet this technique of unmetered rhyming and variable line breaking is clearly imitable, is indeed one of the major stylistic innovations of the twentieth century. The number of free verse poems on this model (a model not, of course, of Logan's devising) is already great, and in itself evidence that rhyme, far from having begun to perish, has undergone important (all but unrecognized) changes.

If we will listen for rhyme and rhyme-related parallelism in much free verse, we will be amazed at the richness and variety of what we hear. The more so because, as Paul Kiparsky has noted, "where parallelism is used as a free feature it is always essential to the meaning . . .; 'free verse' actually frees verse schemas for significant use; hence it can be a more difficult and more expressive form than regulated verse."[88] Rhyme as instance, cut free from larger designs, would appear to have—"always," according to this linguist—full semantic justification, as indeed it does in W. S. Merwin's brief "Homeland":

> The sky goes on living it goes
> on living the sky
> with all the barbed wire of the west
> in its veins
> and the sun goes down
> driving a stake
> through the black heart of Andrew Jackson[89]

A detestation of Jackson is carried by the mocking of his name by harsh rhyme sounds twice in two lines. There is another use of rhyme as a free feature, much more common in free verse than in conventional, and far more likely to produce semantic relationships between rhyme words. A version of this occurs at the middle transition in Hopkins's choral song, when rhymes are conceived as replying to each other, like echoes:

THE LEADEN ECHO

> . . . So be beginning, be beginning to despair.
> O there's none; no no no there's none:
> Be beginning to despair, to despair,
> Despair, despair, despair, despair.

THE GOLDEN ECHO

> Spare!
> There is one, yet I have one (Hush there!). . . .[90]

The second, echoing word is drawn from a nest of associations within the first, and either extends or, as in "despair-spare," denies the first word's logic. It is a strategy of addition, correction, or reversal, where the poet combs out a word's rhyming associations and lays them alongside one another. "There is no direction," writes W. C. Williams in *Paterson*:

> Whither, I
> cannot say. I cannot say
> more than how. The how (the howl) only
> is at my disposal (proposal). . . .

Or again: "with the roar of the river / forever in our ears (arrears)."[91] The rhyme follows its fellow, transforming and extending semantic context. A related method has been used to suggest how the mind races out of control, making metonymic connections along the lines of the rhymes, plunging into language pathology:

> The sky is pitiless. I beg
> your pardon? OK then
> the sky is pitted . . .
>   Yesterday the
> air was squeaky clean today
> it's dull and lifeless as an
> addict's armpit. Surely you mean
> leafless. . . .
>   Some words
> are briefly worse than others:
> get the librium gun and point
> it and Kodak at that Kodiak.
> You see: No hope. So don't
> hope. Hop, skip, jump, or
> lie down. . . .[92]

James Schuyler, author of these lines, clearly knows (with Freud) that double talk is a special form of communication.

From Eliot and MacDiarmid to Schuyler, these examples may remind us how Keats as a child would reply to people by making a rhyme on their sentences, and then laugh.[93] As a language habit, rhyme seems a derangement, seems to say something only about language, but there is always the possibility that it is also telling us something about ourselves. Modern use of the device, on the showing of these passages, may be said to force its artificiality and irrationality into the light. For poet and critic, this can be instructive: when we perceive that language, like nature in the scientist's estimation, is only partially organized, we regain incentive for basic discoveries.

By boycotting puns and confining rhymes, English neoclassical poets wished to control this subversive likelihood of hidden perspectives within language and ourselves. The consciously unified period style of Pope, Swift, and Johnson is the historical opposite of the stylistic pluralism of the post-Romantic era, and hence its abiding attraction. Those twentieth-century poets and critics who promote the chastening lesson of neoclassical examples seem partially to contravene the terrorist imperative of Rimbaud, "One must be absolutely modern." To concentrate intensively on the relation of rhyme to reason is their way of modifying the Romantic frame of mind these writers share with Rimbaud; critics like W. K. Wimsatt argue their particular modernity by insisting that there is more to rhyme than the reverberations of harmonious unreason. Faced with these two modernities, that of Rimbaud and that of Wimsatt, I should like to suggest that each requires the other for its completion.

3: Modernity and Literary Convention

The idea of *modernity* possesses a stronger sense than that of *contemporaneity*, because the former helps us to describe a literary-historical period and also the larger culture of that period. Modernity also does more work for us than *Modernism*, the related but more restrictive term. Modernism is a stylistic category, historically contained, by and large, within the years 1910–1945; it refers to "the radical definition of the medium, its legitimate operations and their scope."[1] Now that modernism is itself history, we require an account of how its forms and themes have their place within the sweep of literary history, at least since the first generation of Romantic writers. So far, my own account has de-emphasized the shift at 1910 in order to claim that the poetics of the whole period since 1795 have been, on a broad front, organicist, with roots in the practice of Wordsworth and Coleridge, and also in the aesthetic theory of Hegel. To take this further, the final chapter will examine the conventionality of literary conventions in the era of modernity. Here as before, rhyme remains the representative device.

This description of the cultural-historical context of literary convention must be tentative, especially when I have ventured to include remarks on Chinese as well as English and

American literature. As I have said in the Preface, this essay foresees a unified field theory of literary equivalences, one that would be historical as well as structural. I believe that to anticipate such a theory we should look beyond this or that culture, this or that single device, so we will be able to examine the very process of making and breaking formal rules under conditions of modernity. The very breadth of my hypothesis makes it debatable; I am aware it cannot be proved decisively with the statements and examples adduced here as cultural analogues. Yet the evidences I have been able to gather do have their degree of pertinence, for they tend to show that, in their statements and their poetic practice, modern poets East and West seek the unattainable ideal condition of organic form. These poets accordingly de-emphasize the institutional elements in the poem: language itself, prosodic systems traditionally defined, rhyme, syntax.

My hypothesis is that the antirhetorical frame of mind is homogeneous and cosmopolitan, occurring as a leap to avant-gardist intelligence in the West about 1795 and in China after the May 4th Movement of 1919. This frame of mind involves the renewing of poetic devices by distortion or omission—and also the renewing of literary and cultural heritages by the processes of translation. Thus the line of Whitman in the hands of Kuo Mo-jo, the elements of accentual-syllabic iambic meter as used by Hsü Chih-mo, the sonnet form as filled in by Feng Chih, though outmoded husks for many native writers of English, become innovative principles in Chinese poetry; as does the Chinese manner of proceeding in English, after Ezra Pound's *Cathay* translations. In these transactions, the specific literary conventions chosen and their origins, even the degree of exactness of the imitation, seem immaterial; what matters is that the émigré format is palpably different from the existing, traditional one. Incredibly, from the perspective of Chinese classical poetry, the sonnet in Chinese may seem a direct and genuine experience.

One of the things which makes modern writing in any language difficult is the vehemence with which our writers themselves formulate rules against the formulation of rules. Some students of the modern period have seen this contradiction of convention as a logical impasse, and thus the proper termination of an inquiry that, in any event, began with a preference for earlier, more elegant texts. However, I choose to take modernity's professed aversion to history and to the institution of literature as my starting point. I understand modernity's position as a form of paradoxical communication and an arraying of strategic overstatements that are deployed either to foster or to protect literary innovation.

The literary scholar is especially concerned with the sort of absolutist demand on language made, for instance, by Rimbaud in his absurd and splendid sonnet proposing the color audition of French vowels. Another instance: Feng Chih in these translated lines from a Chinese sonnet published in 1941:

> From a pool of freely-flowing, formless water,
> The water carrier brings back a bottleful, ellipsoid in shape,
> Thus this much water has acquired a definite form.
> Look, the wind vane fluttering in the autumn breeze
>
> Takes hold of certain things that cannot be held. . . .
> Let's hope that these verses will, like a wind cone,
> Embody certain things that cannot be held.[2]

Though flow theories are not morphological, the modern writer persists in hoping, with Feng Chih, that experience can be conveyed directly, without analysis, in the "definite form" of the text. And that form, since mind is shapely, will embody by analogy certain forms of experience, the very contours of water and wind. Or again, as Walt Whitman argues in his 1855 preface to *Leaves of Grass*, it will be a form as inevitable and organic as a rounded fruit: "The rhyme and uniformity of perfect poems show the free growth of metrical laws and bud from them as unerringly and loosely as lilacs or roses on a bush, and takes shapes as compact as the shapes of chestnuts and oranges and melons and pears, and shed the perfume impalpable to form."[3] The corollary of this, for Whitman, is the extreme assertion that the reader has to deal not only with a book but also with a speaking person who can embrace and be embraced. Thus do Whitman's poems pretend to be experiences unmediated by language: the leaves of a book by metonymy become as direct and unlinguistic as the leaves of the grass in nature. This assimilation of the poem to nature is often, I believe, taken to be an extravagant gesture. That it is not so understood by writers themselves I can demonstrate with ideas on poetic language from highly sophisticated poets: I take their remarks from the personal statements in Wai-lim Yip's anthology of recent poetry from the Republic of China:

> Ya Hsien: "in one sentence, I want to gulp down all the complex variegation in one's sensibility—I become so covetous that I can hardly get a focus."
> Pai Ch'iu: "to remold, as in the fashioning of a handful of clay, and to reorganize into a new mode all the words, ancient and modern, and their combinations . . ."
> Chi Hung: "What I mean by 'giving-forth' in terms of directness and exactness is reproducing through objects and events the complete form received by the heart."
> Chang Mo: "There is no fixed form, language, or technique that can yoke modern poetry. The perspective of modern poetry is built upon its vast and endless change."
> Ch'in Tzu-Hao: "Style is the poet's own voice."
> Hsin Yü: "The true countenance of the hidden objects cannot be brought to light except through new expressions."[4]

Such statements from the recent past demonstrate that Whitman's way of speaking is not outmoded, and begin to suggest a certain logic in his position.

Since that logic is one of the essential keys to modernity's frame of mind, exposing as it does the awareness of an aching distance between language and world, between signifier and signified, I quote from Wai-lim Yip's anthology these revealing lines from near the end of his own poem, "Fugue":

> We have ourselves admired
> Millions of flowers trees bays and waters
> What can we make of the world?
>   We have again come across
> Rimes meters rhythms tones ballads etc.
> What can we make of the world?

Like Walt Whitman and the others quoted, Yip perceives a disproportion between rhetoric and reality. Language, even art language, is seen to be anamorphic with the world, and the modern writer's absolutist statements on the assimilation of poetry to nature are therefore to be taken as implicit commentary on the limits of language. These statements are the honest admission of a deficiency and the extravagant expression of its correction. Human language cannot compass what Yip elsewhere in "Fugue" describes as "the speech of cliffs . . . the hurrah of the sea," yet such a language of the world, if it were possible, would not be memoried or self-reflective. No, the interest of ordinary sentences and art sentences is that at some level we continually perceive them to be models of reality, and as models, susceptible either of precise or of imprecise handling. I imagine this is what Huang Yung means in his statement in the Yip anthology when he remarks that modern poetry "does not search for . . . inaccessible permanence and universality, it aims at the release of its character"[5] —a character, I may add, fashioned like language itself by objective and subjective determinants.

Until now I have been concerned with poetic statements of belief, with programs and manifestos. In the West, and also in the Oriental literatures, the leading mode for pronouncements on poetics in the classical era was the handbook or manual: a body of descriptive poetics which insensibly and in the course of time became prescriptive. In the modern period it would appear that poetics resides largely in the more strident form of the manifesto, whose aim is to separate the poet or his group from all those others past and present who can be maligned as "The Traditionalists of Plagiarism" (in a phrase from W. C. Williams). Blake's condemnation of Bysshe and the handbooks of Augustan form, Wordsworth's preface of 1800 and Whitman's of 1855, Pound's "A Few Donts by an Imagist" of 1913, Hu Shih's eight antitraditionalist "Donts" of 1916, the polemic surrounding the adoption of free verse and colloquial language after China's May 4th Movement of 1919, the statements in the Yip anthology—these are the utterances of writers without a handbook or the authority of a period style. These writers work by hypotheses stated as assertions, by negative injunctions, avoidances. Creation occurs in the context of a series of provisional hypotheses about the meaning of meter, rhythm, and the nature of art language. The manifestos are histrionic and heuristic. They dare and supplicate the reader as they project into the future a schedule and strategy for personal work. And if, for the writer, they define a field of action, for the reader they afford a gesture of solidarity, suggesting what lenses are necessary for appreciation of the work. Thus to read these productions in a univocal way, to be insulted by them, or to disregard them completely as oversimplifications, is to misunderstand their nature. They are in fact clues, historical and methodological study guides to aid us in our task of reading.

Once we have understood the manifesto as the expression of a hope and the description of a theoretical limit, we are prepared to take seriously those metaphors of organic form which are a sign of avant-gardist intentions whatever their national origin. Except among poets and their manifestos, our century's thinking on poetic form has been notably wary of "organic-form" theories of the poem's construction. Critics have argued that such theories are naive in their understanding of language and of artistic convention; it has been noted that crude theories of this sort deprive the poet of any active choice in how the poem is made, for he escapes that "anxiety of influence" (Harold Bloom) which received language and its many conventions carry as a necessity. An American student of American criticism, Murray Krieger, poses a typical question: "What can a theory do to help us toward relating rhetoric and poetic when it rests on the need to denigrate rhetoric in order to create the very possibility of poetry?"[6] That question forms the crux in any discussion of device and modernity, the opening and not the end point of debate. Of course, insofar as we want to do literary history seriously, we are all antimodern moderns; yet some are more anxious than others about the organic hypothesis and its validity.

Avoiding all unsubtle formulation that would oppose rhetoric to spontaneity, Coleridge insists: "Imagine not I am about to oppose genius to rules. No! the comparative value of these rules is the very cause to be tried."[7] Coleridge, who disagreed with Wordsworth's reckless formulation of a vernacular poetry as the "real" language of men, knows there is no choice whether or not to use rhetorical heightening; the poet's only choice is of the kind of rhetoric he will use. With the first Romantic generation begins the systematic search for those conventions that will best enact the illusion of spontaneity. Romantic and avant-gardist poetics are concerned with the historical constraints upon conventions, when these constraints are defined always as causes "to be tried." Rhetoric is never abandoned, merely seen as provisional.

It is possible, in fact, that the choice between the principles of organic form and of analysis is not genuine. First, because, to a large extent, all who come after the Romantic writers in the West, or after the leap to modernism in the China of 1919, have absorbed the organicist way of thinking and necessarily exemplify it in arguments. Those who, for example, argue that the premises of organic form, when we come down to study the poem in detail, really are nothing more than immemorial Aristotelian (or Confucian) notions with new terms as guises, are either denying their own moment in history, their own modernity; or else they are stealthy organicists in their ambivalence toward the verbal icon.[8] Something constitutive and unprecedented occurred in the West around 1795, just as in China, during 1919: the inauguration of a language of the destruction of language, and of a literature of the salutary depreciation of literature. A second reason for the conceptual priority of theories of organic form lies in the notion that the descriptive-analytical approach can be immediately derived from the organic one, but not conversely. Hierarchies and inventories of elements and devices can be derived, at various levels, from the more encompassing system with its full complement of generative rules and principles. "The choice . . . is not between two competing grammars, but between a grammar and one particular aspect of that grammar": thus Noam Chomsky on the two traditions in modern linguistic theory, the universal and the structural or descriptive. I believe a very similar case may be made for synthesis in literary history and methodology.[9]

This may be possible if we proceed within the framework of cognitive psychology and open our studies to history and to the insights of linguistics, gestalt psychology, and alternate concepts of logic, method, and structure. Much of the present study is devoted to returning the poetic technique or device to the movement of the line and of the poem as a whole, and to returning the poem to its special historical moment. By precise dating we make explicit the function of the device in its historical time, and as testimony of that time. We need to remember, perhaps, in this kind of project, that the antirhetorical, antihistorical way of talking in modernity's manifestos is itself determined by history. Modernity and the theory of organic form require each other: they did not converge and become synonymous by accident, but are part of the same historical moment. To return the device to the poem and to history is therefore not (or not only) the accommodation, or the restraining, of an innovative literature, but rather a collaboration with that literature, a completion.

MODERNITY AND PERIODIZATION

Etymologically the *rhetor* is a public speaker. Historically, rhetoric in its judicial, forensic, deliberative, and demonstrative forms was prose discourse intended to influence judgment; a technique of argument, then, not of ornamentation. But in the West, rhetoric, as a means of controlling the auditor by polished language, very early became the object of moral disapproval. What if a liar developed verbal resourcefulness? And so the fortunes, indeed the very meaning of rhetoric have fluctuated: from Aristotle and Quintilian down to the structuralist of the present day, writers have been anxious to clear the name of rhetoric. That task may be an impossible one, now that normative rhetoric in our period has taken on the meaning of nonpoetry, the kind of literary eloquence that, Verlaine said, should have its neck wrung.[10]

But it was not always thus: rhetoric was once identical with poetry. In the European Middle Ages, when rhetoric, grammar, and logic composed the trivium of study, the fusion of rhetoric and poetic was virtually complete; this was true also in theory and practice in China, for instance, during the Sung dynasty.[11] During the next centuries in Europe there occurred a steady widening of the definition thus subsuming grammar and logic, and there developed a new emphasis on manipulating the traditional figures as coded in manuals. Critical theory in such periods is inevitably moral and psychological. For many centuries in China the short poem was not only a literary norm—excellence in its composition was almost the only passport to ruling-class careers; and during the longest reign of any period style in English, the heroic couplet between 1660 and 1795 was promoted over every alternate form. Partly because of the restrictions of the twenty-syllable cage of the couplet, writers during this time in England elaborated a special literary language or poetic diction, similar to China's literary dialect (*wen-yen*) but less systematic.

Suddenly, and correlating very precisely to a shift in the economic and political base, a sharp break occurs, a literary

revolution in whose field of influence we still exist. With
Wordsworth and Coleridge as with Hu Shih and Kuo Mo-jo,
rhetoric is renounced, or, more precisely, seen to be expenda-
ble. (Though in England [1795] and China [1919] there then
came on the scene writers who with no philosophic depth at
all contrasted rhetoric with "reality," I am here concerned
only with showing what is major and exemplary.) Suddenly
the centuries-old structure is unroofed: Thomas DeQuincey,
commenting on a new age of social and literary pluralism,
said in 1828: "the age of Rhetoric, like that of Chivalry, has
passed amongst forgotten things."[12] The speed and violence
of the change is even greater in China after the May 4th
Movement, and yet the attributes of the new literature are the
same as in the West: the complete replacement of the literary
language by the vernacular; a weakening of shape accom-
panied by an emphasis on new patterns of measuring, which
leads eventually in both literatures to free verse; the substitution of what Coleridge called "form as proceeding" for
"shape as superinduced" as an account of poetic movement;
the critical strategy, already discussed, of assimilating poetry
to natural forms and processes; and the emergence of a stylistic pluralism where many types of writing are possible—
including the classical mode of the previous era. But no one
type predominates. It is important to recognize just what a
quantum leap is contained in the critical premises of the
Romantic movement. Wordsworth's assertion that in his
poetry emotion and feeling give importance to action, instead
of the other way around, as well as his claim that he hopes to
create the taste by which his poetry will be enjoyed, are out-
ward signs not of variation but of powerful innovation. And
these claims, which can be matched in Whitman, in Kuo Mo-
jo and Wen I-to, are phrased in a subjectivistic critical
vocabulary that consciously denies the more prescriptive poetics of the manuals.

After 1795 every element of the text must be charged with

that specific and quasi-physiological selfhood we now call "style," a middle-class phenomenon, as Fredric Jameson has described it, which "reflects the increasing atomization of middle-class life": and which always represents "an individual and problematical solution to the dilemma of the absence of a public."[13] Style emerges "from the silence of the isolated individual," and its coming manifests the contradictions of a new historical period, a separation from the historical domain of rhetoric. In Jameson's description: "Rhetoric is an older and essentially pre-capitalist mode of linguistic organization . . . a collective or class phenomenon, in that it serves as a means of assimilating the speech of individuals to some suprapersonal or oratorical paradigm, to some non or pre-individualistic standard . . . of high style and fine writing." Of course, so long as we possess and read the texts of the rhetorical mode, this mode will always have a true currency in those writings. What is lost is not the mode itself, but its rationale, its authority. With respect to the special techniques of prosody, a device such as rhyme, meter, or metaphor will indeed reappear after the shift to the mode of style, yet with its function and meaning changed: reinvented, as it were, from within.

A dominant premise of the rhetorical mode is "nature," yet accompanying every usage of this term of praise is the unwritten subscript: "Nature = Art." For the classicist the concept of nature is itself a projection of the prescriptive conventions called rules. In the aesthetics of the West, the Nature = Art equation is seen by the emergent Romantics to be a spurious way of claiming that historically determined styles and devices are natural growths, and as a consequence the Romantic movement (as Harry Levin says) "drew its heavy line between the artificial and the natural."[14] In an essay that marvelously extends Levin's insight, Claudio Guillén has described how poetic conventions "were fully recognized for the first time by the cultural movement which had begun by estranging itself from them" in its reaction against neoclassical poetics.

Romantic and avant-gardist poetics had, in fact, "no genuine quarrel with conventions, without which it would not be possible to draw the necessary line between the poetic and the natural."[15] When rhetoric became the intentional image of the Romantic self, the portcullis of history closed upon a historical domain. And because a period could be seen to have closed definitively, literary history became possible—in the sense of the organization of the past and the arrangement of classification systems for the study of period styles. I have located this epistemological-prosodic break, for Europe, around 1795; for China, in 1919. At both these times the decline of a traditional form of writing in a highly specialized language corresponds with the fall of a type of society. Leo Ou-fan Lee's recent book on Hsü Chih-mo, Kuo Mo-jo, and three others makes the historical affiliation explicit, calling these men the Romantic generation of modern Chinese writers.[16]

The history of literature, with its own complex of structural laws, is always linked to other historical sequences, but at no time more intimately (or obviously) than during such a break or eruption. At these moments literature seems to invade non-literature, and writers feel their lives to be intensely historical. In Wordsworth, in Kuo Mo-jo, literature intersects politics in the theme of revolution. At a slightly later date there come onto the European and Chinese scenes those societies and journals of avant-gardism whose names suggest historical placement and literary innovation: *Broom, Vortex,* The Creation Society, *Origin,* and *Epoch Poetry Quarterly.* With few exceptions, even the best modern studies of periodization tend to avoid this concept of a break in historical continuity. Claudio Guillén discusses, as limiting instances, a dynamic period dating belonging to liberal personalities and reformers, and at the opposite extreme a type of history which emphasizes discontinuous structures and provides us with "eternal 'presents' in the past."[17] But there is no provision in his scale for a qualitative historical distinction between before and after, when the latter would describe the *raison d'être* of any and all styles in the avant-garde period. That the leap to modernity is similar in its themes in both Europe and the East is only one of the aspects of such a model which commends to the scholar its power of explanation. After 1919 China compressed into fewer than ten years all those aspects and phases of the avant-garde—the resort to the colloquial, the development of free verse, nihilism, agonism, and so on—which took fifty or a hundred years to be played out in Europe, and this because (as Bonnie S. McDougall has shown in detail) China had vividly before it the example of Europe.[18] Chow Tsetung, the historian of this twentieth century intellectual revolution, says of the May 4th Movement that it "shook China to her roots and . . . after forty years [1960], is still reverberating."[19] The concept of a literary period does not correspond to a historical fact but rather answers a need, creates a mode of understanding for the historian. Why have commentators on Romanticism preferred to see it as one undulation among many, rather than a tidal wave? One corrective might be the development, in literary studies, of a plausible theory of continuity through revolution.[20]

If the notion of a "break" seems imprudent, perhaps we will at least term this phenomenon the development of an anxiety, a contagion of dubiety which infects writers (and their commentators) to the degree that they are fully aware of the provisional quality of all rhetorics in the modern period. After all, the new domain of modernity is related to the previous domain by dialectical structures of reversal and dispersion, and, from another perspective, is not so much a break as a giddy acceleration of processes of stylistic dynamism and linguistic self-reflexiveness already present. To adopt even this weaker position is still, inevitably, to challenge an extant account of period styles which prizes continuity over discontinuity, and which tends to detach literary history from general history because of the alleged autonomy, the supra-temporal dimension, of literature. Yet an exact dating of poems and their devices cannot coexist with a model of literary history containing an assumption of literature's transhistorical status.

FORM AS TRANSGRESSION

The modern writer's search for what Geoffrey Hartman has called the "unmediated vision," where nature, the body, and human consciousness would be the only text, has made the idea of literature seem incompatible with the idea of modernity.[21] If we as commentators isolate the absolutist impulse in our literature, understanding its permanent heterodoxy as permanent revolution, we find it impossible to write the history of antihistorical objects. Or so it appears if we accept the strategic hyperboles and manifestos as brute data. However, once we understand the avant-gardist statements as expressions of a limiting case, a hope and a direction, we understand avant-gardism not as the abrogation of language but as a decisive realignment of its table of values. Our writers, that is, are finally aware that counterconvention is, or quickly becomes, itself a convention: today's demonic style is tomorrow's accepted mode. The poet knows *but does not acknowledge* a mediator for his orphic journey. The nonrecognition protects his talent and his need to remake language, while the intuition sensibly certifies, in the words of Gérard Genette, that "a personal creation in the strong sense does not exist . . . because literary practice takes place as a vast *combinatory* game within a pre-existing system which is none other than language itself. . . . A new creation is usually nothing but the chance encounter with a blank space (if one remains) in the table of forms, and consequently the constant desire to innovate by marking oneself off from one's predecessors . . . rests on a naive illusion."[22] Naive but, it may be, necessary: the antirhetorical intelligence is tenacious, and will be a feature of literary debate until the avant-garde is itself surpassed. It is worth noting that recently the avant-garde proved itself alive and well by the invention of a new period concept, post-modernism, to describe the phase in the tradition of the new in which we have our being and create texts.[23] Not even a popular and journalistic acceptance of avant-garde writing as the major literature of our time has diminished the need for statements proclaiming absolute rather than partial innovation.

In the China of the twenties, as earlier in the West, poets seem to have believed that when they converted from the literary dialect to the vernacular, poems would write themselves. After the original enthusiasm it became evident that there was still an obligation to work the vernacular itself into art sentences. Accordingly we find more variety, more delicacy, in the free rhythms of W. C. Williams and Wai-lim Yip than in those of Walt Whitman and Kuo Mo-jo. In the modern period no specific device of equivalence, neither meter nor rhyme nor metaphor nor parallelism, is required: the only requirement existing is that the chosen device be "reinvented," in the sense of being used to express, as far as possible, the very feeling tones of the writer. All devices are simultaneously necessary and dispensable. Further, if all literary art performs what Roland Barthes calls "defections from the semantic system," "creative transgressions" from ordinary language, modern writing with its essentialist ambitions goes further—actually uses language in the attempt to murder language.[24] If all art language makes departures from normal usage, overdetermining syntax with an extra richness of parallelism, modern art sentences will seek outrageous or untried patterns in the table of forms, or indeed import a new table of forms of equivalence.

Yeats, describing his youthful poem "The Lake Isle of Innisfree" in his *Autobiography*, says he had, at the time of writing, begun to "loosen rhythm as an escape from rhetoric and from that emotion of the crowd rhetoric brings," but he did not fully understand that he must "use nothing but the common syntax." A "couple of years later," he says, "I would not have written that first line with its conventional archaism —'Arise and go'—nor the inversion in the last stanza ['the pavements gray']."[25] Along the same line, Sylvia Plath had written, in her draft:

> Gentlemen, ladies
>
> These are my hands
> My knees.
> I may be skin and bone,
> *I may be Japanese . . .*

In his memoir of Plath, Alvarez says he "niggled away at her. 'Do you just need the rhyme? Or are you trying to hitch an easy lift by dragging in the atomic victims? If you're going to use this kind of violent material, you've got to play it cool.'" Plath had "argued back sharply," but in the poem as published after her death the line in question had been dropped, and Alvarez, commenting later, writes "that . . . is a pity: she did need the rhyme. . . . I was overreacting to the initial brutality of the verse without understanding its weird elegance."[26] Rather understate than otherwise: thus our bad conscience with respect to the device. Why else was Ezra Pound possessed by the scholarly despair of the latecomer when he tried to translate the Provençal *canzon*? That abundance of rhymes intricately interlaced was, he knew, strictly untranslatable and inimitable. If once, in the poetry of the High Middle Ages, perhaps in the T'ang dynasty in China, the form seemed transparent, that marvelous and perhaps imagined moment had passed, to remain vivid only as an ideal of organic form, a theoretical limit.

In a note "On Open Form," the American poet W. S. Merwin has very exactly phrased the post-Romantic and Poundian historical recognitions:

The invention of a new form of stanza was a matter of genuine poetic importance to the troubadours. . . . For [them] the abstract form (which certainly they did not hear as an abstract thing) was unquestionably related to that part of the poem that was poetic. For us, it is hard to remain convinced that the form, insofar as it is abstract, is not merely part of what in the poem is inescapably technical. For us, for whom everything is in question, the making keeps leading us back into the patterns of a world of artifice so intricate, so insidious, and so impressive, that often it seems indistinguishable from the whole of time.[27]

In our period, as in all others, a device may be passionately embraced and dismissed within the same generation, often within the work of one writer; and now as before there is admiration for an earlier, freer technique, for a time when form was friendly. However, we are those "for whom everything is in question": now all writers are dubious of the ability of devices to carry meaning. If Pound reveres Arnaut Daniel and Dante; Merwin, the Arcipreste de Hita, Guillaume de Lorris, and Chaucer; if Wai-lim Yip says we must learn from Wang Wei, that kind of admiration is consciously historical and refuses to assimilate historical styles into natural growths. I emphasize the lack of exceptions to the sense that poetic devices are verbal icons, and as such regrettable and strictly necessary. The point is worth repeating, because the general necessity of having devices to insure art speech can all but camouflage the dispensability of any particular device in a particular poem. Prosody is of itself a system that can be used to divert attention (the poet's, the reader's) from an inherited modern intelligence, because this is a "world of artifice so intricate, so insidious, and so impressive" that it may appear independent of history. The fact is that some avant-gardist writers since Wordsworth, since Hu Shih, have a higher innovational ratio than others. But those others are not exempt from history merely because, like Wen I-to, or W. H. Auden, or Robert Frost, they often write in impeccable stanza forms and measure their lines in a familiar way.

Consider, for an excellent example of how styles and devices date themselves, Wen I-to's famous early modernist poem "The Dead Water" (1926).

Here is a ditch of hopelessly dead water.
No breeze can raise a single ripple on it.
Might as well throw in rusty metal scraps
or even pour left-over food and soup in it.

Perhaps the green on copper will become emeralds.
Perhaps on tin cans peach blossoms will bloom.
Then, let grease weave a layer of silky gauze,
and germs brew patches of colorful spume.

Let the dead water ferment into jade wine
covered with floating pearls of white scum.
Small pearls chuckle and become big pearls,
only to burst as gnats come to steal this rum.

And so this ditch of hopelessly dead water
may still claim a touch of something bright.
And if the frogs cannot bear the silence—
the dead water will croak its song of delight.

Here is a ditch of hopelessly dead water—
a region where beauty can never reside.
Might as well let the devil cultivate it—
and see what sort of world it can provide.[28]

In the original this bears many of the marks of classical Chinese poetry: lines contain equal numbers of characters and are divided into traditional quatrains by the device of end rhyme (*abcb*); and a proportion of the imagery is conventional in its references to jadeite, peachblossoms, silk, pearls. However the poem speaks the moment of its construction very precisely in rhythm, sound, and appearance; it could never be mistaken for a poem written in the T'ang style because it is cast in the vernacular (called *pai hua*), and it pointedly avoids the literary dialect. In every line there is a system of other avoidances. Whereas the classical line employed five to seven characters, Wen I-to has here created a nine character sequence divided into four groups: three of two syllables and one of three syllables, with the three-syllable group changing its position through successive lines as a way to defeat monotony.[29] By such construction the poet is able to work up a rich texture of disyllabic compounds, chastening the tendency of *pai hua* to multiply loose monosyllables while, at the same time, stretching the line beyond the cognitive and prosodic "depth" of the classical expectation.

The second stanza is perhaps the finest, and I offer it here in a literal translation that shows the placement of characters in the line and the syllable groupings (/) as Cyril Birch has determined them:[30]

也	許	銅	的	要	緑	成	翡	翠
yeh	hsü /	t'ung	te	yao /	lü	ch'eng /	fei	ts'ui
perhaps	———	bronze	(poss.)	will	green	into	jadeite	———

鐵	罐	上	銹	出	幾	瓣	桃	花
t'ieh	kuan	shang /	hsiu	ch'u /	chi	pan /	t'ao	hua
iron	can	on	rust (v.)	out	some	petals of	peach	blossom

再	讓	油	膩	織	一	層	羅	綺
tsai	jang /	yu	ni /	chih	i	ts'eng /	lo	ch'i
further	let	oil	grease	weave	one	layer of	silk	———

黴	菌	給	他	蒸	出	些	雲	霞
mei	chün /	ke	t'a /	cheng	ch'u /	hsieh /	yün	hsia
mold	fungus	for	him	steam	out	some	clouds	colored
			(water)	(v.)				clouds

The tone of bitterness is conveyed by the images. Here, as throughout the poem, everything that is degenerate, viscous, and sordid is transformed to a bright semblance—beauty of pearls or jade, which might seem appropriate to a traditional Chinese poem until we remember its origins in the "ditch of disillusioned dead water" (line 1). Sickened with himself, and perhaps too with a China torn by civil war and invaded from without, Wen I-to manifests the contradictions of a historical moment by projecting a sardonic desolation onto things seen. In this historical setting, it seems imaginative literature is justifiable only as an urban, Baudelairean flower of evil. Prosody, imagery, and theme all manifest the contradictions of an evil time.

It would have been possible to inspect free verse poems from the same period in China, but I think less informative. The value of the Wen I-to poem, what I call its faint modernism, is its unwillingness to be extravagantly violent. For Wen I-to, as for many Chinese and American poets of the present day, there is no need to abolish rhyme: "not to use it," he said, "would be like starving in front of a royal banquet."[31] He knows, I think, that the use of *pai hua* and the lengthening of the line and the confrontation of traditional with sordid images are themselves sufficient to certify modernity. Wen I-to's practice converges with the contemporaneous work, in the twenties, of the Russian Formalists, whose focus on what automatizes the word and the device, making the sense of reality disappear, created a link between literary theory and practice. The critic's question, like the poet's, is: What configuration of lively language will make the world, as mediated in the work of art, lose its automatic familiarity and, estranging itself, become perceptible? Then as now, as the poets have known, we need a historical and psychological study of devices that, as trammels and constraints, flaunt their literariness: which are the material condition of all verbal art, but which (by their boldness in overdetermining language) defy our post-Romantic norms, our myth of an imaginary organic form.

THE BLANK SPACES IN THE TABLE OF FORMS

Post-Romantic writers are suspicious of literary form in its guise of ornamental rhetoric, and this has made the history and role of the device central in modern poetics. Rhyme, the instance chosen, is not disappearing in English and American poetry, but rather is being wrenched as far as possible into personal meaning. To defeat expectation, the device is warped, re-positioned, used as instance rather than design in unmetered poems with variable line breaking. In history and in cognition these distortions of rhyme correlate it with free verse—which places unexpectedly heavy reliance on rhyme, but only to de-emphasize its traditional role as a marker of literariness. Successful use of rhyme as a free feature has altered rhyme's meaning, and yet this resource will not be extinguished: modern rhyme still exemplifies the ancient dynamic whereby two meanings find the same sound.

My description of post-Romantic rhyme, as the selection of unfamiliar forms of the device which will certify spontaneity, matches Paul de Man's account of the modernity of a literary period "as the manner in which it discovers the impossibility of being modern."[32] Device and modernity are paradoxical formulations, united in a rapport-of-difference, the one standing for a false bondage to convention, and the other standing for a false detachment from it. When we apprehend the poem as a historical utterance, we surpass these difficulties in the experience of reading. "The spontaneity of being modern conflicts with the claim to think and write about modernity," writes de Man: "it is not at all certain that literature and modernity are in any way compatible concepts." Into that sentence place "device" as subscript for "literature" to specify the term, and "history" above it to raise it to a higher power, and the project of the present essay is given in brief. The attempt has been to coordinate several concepts by the use of a single, narrowly defined convention of sound and sense. In the instance of rhyme, the terms *device* and *modernity* are not compatible, but rather dialectically related and mutually defining. Perhaps the terms *device* and *modernity* in coordination may, even more successfully than modernity alone in de Man's phrasing, be "one of the ways by means of which the link between literary theory and literary praxis is being partially restored." If such a link is to be salvaged, the exemplary pasages quoted here must by their representative nature carry an especially heavy weight of conviction.

Let us return to a sentence already quoted from Gérard Genette: "A new creation is usually nothing but the chance encounter with a blank space (if one remains) in the table of forms." Conceivably the possibilities for permutation of rhyme could be laid out as a schema of sounds and positions. Many of these options would be foreclosed by previous usage; for example, Wimsattian or "reasonable" rhyme in the stricter Popian model will be a mode admirably achieved in another century and, while always possible, never strongly probable in an age of stylistic pluralism. The rhyming tradition in English is so rich, so formidable, that inevitably the blank spaces on our table will be hard to find and will, this late in history, consist mainly of antirhyme and distortions of canonical rhyme.[33] The encounter with a new rhyme form will not, therefore, be entirely the matter of chance that Genette seems to imply, but neither will it be something dictated by the canon. The off-key consonant rhymes of Dickinson, Owen, Auden, and the later Yeats are clearly deliberate dishevelments, attempts to cut the sound sweetness of most high Victorian rhyme, except Browning's. The placement of rhymes in passages from Logan and Dorn, above, prefigures one kind of sporadic sound linkage that, in time, will perhaps become the norm rather than the deviation.

For a modernist instance, representative in the quality and the placement of its sound repetitions, here is H. D.'s "Oread":

> Whirl up, sea—
> whirl your pointed pines,
> splash your great pines
> on our rocks,
> hurl your green over us
> cover us with your pools of fir.[34]

The tree nymph, speaking, sees the ocean with the imagery of her own forests, and this charming misinterpretation is articulated through words keyed to one another rather as they are in the Logan poem described in chapter two. Several sequences are at work: Whirl-whirl-hurl-fir, your-your, pines-pines, great-green, over-cover, some of these true rhyme or alliteration, others simple repetition. But the linkages of sound do not fall at predictable places in the lines; so, while the little poem is densely packed with devices, they are hardly identified as such. For this reason, the poem, though written more than fifty years ago, is still fresh in its technique. To my mind the same is true of the italicized devices in these passages:

Sumer, nû wil dîn ge*walt*
walt den anger und die *heide*
beide kleiden: dast dien *kleinen* vogeln nôt.[35]

Ich *minne, sinne,* lange *zît*
ver*sinne Minne sich*
wie sie schône lône mîner tage.
Nû *lône schône:* dêst *mîin strît*
vil *kleine meine mich,*
neine meine kleine mîine klage . . .[36]

Bar mîn *herze* ie bernde *wunne,*
daz was *swenne* ich sach ir *wunne*clîchen *schîn*
unde ir *ougen* sam der *sunne*
dur *mîn ougen* liuhten in *daz herze mîn*
dar nâch wart mir leit in kurzen *stunden.*
owê *Minne wunden!*
wie hâst dû dich mîn sus *underwunden*
daz ich sender siecher bin noch fröiden *bar!*[37]

N'onc preterit present n'i *fu*
Et si vous redi que li *fu-*
Turs n'i aura james presence. . . .[38]

Lo mon *veg* cazut *fort* en greu *port* et des*treg*
Quar e p*leg* vol des*cort* e far *tort* contra *dreg* per na*leg*. . . .[39]

Pierre Guiraud, from whom I borrow the French examples, remarks: "It will perhaps seem paradoxical to compare two versifications apparently so opposed: to put face to face modern free verse and the fixed forms of the Middle Ages. However the two techniques proceed from principles partly held in common."[40] Guiraud is able to show that Paul Verlaine, the man who wrote (in a rhyming poem!) that we must wring the neck of rhyme, employs the same sort of witty segmentation of rhyme words ("devant elle-de dentelle") as certain medieval poets. The syllabic breaking of "fu- / Turs" in the *Roman de la Rose* passage is the sort of careful impertinence one would not have thought possible before Apollinaire or Marianne Moore. One may select for notice the rhyming of end words with those at line beginnings, the jamming of equivalences into line middles, the leapfrogging of one rhyme over another, and the eight-line stanza that begins and ends with the same word ("Bar"), thus inordinately stretching the reader's retroactive memory: these techniques achieve a striking modernity of placement, rhythm, and harmony. The passages give force to Guiraud's point that the modern poets, "in breaking the molds of classical rules, within which poetry would have finished by being extinguished, could not help but renew a tradition." The similarities occur because poets who initiate a device are in respect of technique in the same situation as those who have the historical task of reinventing it from within.

Commenting on the Middle High German passages, Henry Lanz notices a certain "absurdity" in Gottfried von Neifen's "complicated rhyming devices," and goes on to say that this proves "there is no natural limit where musical phrases of this kind should begin or stop."[41] Following Jan M. Meijer, I have already shown that rhyme never accelerates or brakes itself but relies for its pace on cognitive principles in the content of the text. Further, to respond to the idea that the very complication of usage indicates the primitive state of medieval rhyme, I should say that rhymes are known to be rhymes, and absurd, successful, reasonable, daring, primitive, only by reference to preexisting conventions that enable us to understand the device in context. In this sense the device has the force of genre; and with medieval as with modern texts, when forms and genres are in flux, it seems best to avoid prescriptive commentary. This is especially true with modern rhyme, where today's extreme distortion is tomorrow's hateful precedent. Modern rhyme exploits a much looser definition of the device and admits within its confines forms of simple repetition already noticed, for example, in passages from Mallarmé, Jarrell, and H. D. This method, much used by our poets for local emphasis, is far closer to homoeoteleuton than to Wimsattian reasonable rhyme, but that is its special, unwitty tone:

'What is that noise?'
                              The wind under the door.
'What is that noise now? What is the wind doing?'
                              Nothing again nothing.
                                                        'Do
'You know nothing? Do you see nothing? Do you
    remember
'Nothing?'[42]

Bavarian gentians, big and dark, only dark
darkening the day time, torch-like with the smoking
        blueness of Pluto's gloom,
ribbed and torch-like, with their blaze of darkness
        spread blue
down flattening into points, flattened under the sweep
        of white day
torch flower of the blue-smoking darkness, Pluto's
        dark-blue daze
black lamps from the halls of Dis, burning dark blue,
giving off darkness, blue darkness, as Demeter's pale
        lamps give off light,
lead me then, lead the way.[43]

From this almost choral return not of ending sounds but identical whole words, the evanescence of the device may be pur-

sued even further. "There are subject-rhymes, two sensibili-
ties may rhyme, there are culture-rhymes," Hugh Kenner
writes helpfully of thematic rhyming in the recurrent topics of
long poems like Pound's *Cantos*, and by now we are entirely
off the table of forms and have begun to use the device as an
analogy.[44] This too modernity includes.

Since the innovative blank spaces occur on a table of
forms, there is no special hierarchy of literary over nonliterary types of rhyming. And this being so, with literary rhyming already covering the table with precedents, it seems more
likely that the most promising area of evolution within the
device will be the sector of ordinary language broadly defined. Ordinary and nonliterary forms will be translated, as
in the Last Poets' shifting of political harangue into drum
chants—or Robert Creeley's sinister rewriting of the tones of
nursery rhyme:

> If you were going to get a pet
> What kind of animal would you get.
>
> A soft bodied dog, a hen—
> feathers and fur to begin it again.
>
> When the sun goes down and it gets dark
> I saw an animal in a park.
>
> Bring it home, to give it to you.
> I have seen animals break in two.[45]

Innovative work will also, very likely, take place in the
border country between poetry and art prose. Poetry will
give alliterative and rhymelike effects to the sequence, fic-
tional or essayistic, of Gertrude Stein and James Joyce,
Charles Olson and Edward Dahlberg; meanwhile prose will
help determine the innovating rhythms of prose poems such
as this fourth of Geoffrey Hill's *Mercian Hymns* (1971):

> I was invested in mother-earth, the crypt of roots
>   and endings. Child's play. I abode there, bided my
>   time: where the mole

> shouldered the clogged wheel, his golden solidus; where
> dry-dust badgers thronged the Roman flues, the
> long-unlooked-for mansions of our tribe.[46]

In the reader's developing apprehension, this physical division of words abutting each other in syntax and linked by rhyme ("mole / shouldered") is eventful, a rhyme through enjambment keyed, below, to the sounds in "gold solidus." The sophisticated mimetic effect achieved by sound and position in "shouldered" fills one blank space in the table of forms. Further, Hill has made play with the most rudimentary form of rhyming in the language, the verb paradigm ("I abode there, bided my time"); and this in a forbidding masterpiece that drives "right down into the gorge of modernism— where," says Calvin Bedient, "the unwritten law is the risk of the greatest chaos that can yet give a poignant hint of a difficult order."[47]

Earlier I used Frost's "Desert Places" as a poem that imitates, and thereby formalizes, the habits of speech. Josephine Miles gives an even more pronounced example of appropriated garrulity, the hoisting of speech acts into complex literariness; the title is "Reason":

> Said, Pull her up a bit will you, Mac, I want to unload there.
> Said, Pull her up my rear end, first come first serve.
> Said, Give her the gun, Bud, he needs a taste of his own bumper.
> Then the usher came out and got into the act:
>
> Said, Pull her up, pull her up a bit, we need this space, sir.
> Said, For God's sake, is this still a free country or what?
> You go back and take care of Gary Cooper's horse
> And leave me handle my own car.
>
> Saw them unloading the lame old lady,
> Ducked out under the wheel and gave her an elbow,
> Said, All you needed to do was just explain;
> *Reason, Reason* is my middle name.[48]

Without a consistent iambic ground pattern or a single conventional rhyme, these lines achieve their own decorum. "The act" (line 4) is palpably a speech act, dramatized conversation, single lines of dialogue arranged to expose character. The speakers are not identified by quotation marks, but eventually the reader sorts out the violent, overinsistent tones of Reason, which prevail at the end just short of physical assault. Having at first bristled at what turned out to be a sensible request, Reason at last accedes and explains with the same theatrical surplus of language; he convicts, then partly redeems himself by his own speech. Mr Reason is, we discover, something less than Reason personified, yet we savor every idiom of his street talk. And what is the relation of rhyme to Reason? Anaphora ("Said") begins six of twelve lines conversationally, binding the discontinuous lines with a rhymelike function. Certain of the repetitions are ironic, like the last line's "*Reason, Reason,*" the name that gives personal as well as general import to the poem's title. In two places the poem verges on traditional rhyme: "car" repeats a consonant from "sir," and the two final lines, verging on iambic pentameter for an effect of closure, are linked by an imperfect rhyme ("Explain-name"). Though Josephine Miles accounts for a trait of character through representation of idiomatic voice, and thus cannot let the literariness of bold devices obtrude, she leads her readers to the point where we are content to let rhyme be her conclusion.

THE FORTUITOUSNESS OF ART

To think about the relation of device and modernity is to concern oneself with the definition of the poet's free will. This freedom appears to be a vivid margin or growing edge, moving slightly beyond the limitations of the language material and the historical moment. Every "chance encounter with a blank space . . . in the table of forms" is itself structurally and historically determined by those limits, and in turn redefines those limits. Wishing to neglect neither the fortuitousness nor the determinateness of art, we are bound to step back, at times in the inquiry, to see how our "acquisitions in synchronic concept oblige us to re-examine the principles of diachrony."[49] Thus the words of Tynjanov and Jakobson, who describe, in their theses on literary evolution, how the purely ahistorical concept discovers itself to be an illusion, and next discovers that "the history of the system is in its turn a system." It is at this point that author's styles and period styles are folded back into literary history, and literary history itself related to "other historical series: each of these series consists of a complex bundle of structural laws appropriate to it." The mediations between the literary and historical series after 1795 are impossible to trace, here, in their full detail; yet I would mention the inseparability, after this date, of stylistic pluralism in the literary series and ethical alienation in the historical series. The post-Romantic avant-gardist moment is one of severely decreased ethical and stylistic authority, and is, through mediations, dependent on the historical base in an era of technological and bourgeois revolutions. Any future accomplishment of a unified period style, like the one that obtained in English poetry between 1660 and 1795, will be strictly impossible without a prior change in the historical series.

Yet many persons will nonetheless frame to themselves the stylistic conditions of authority which will obtain after such a period style is achieved. Modern Aristotelian critics have made a strong exposition of the centrality of rhetoric, the quiddity of the device, the need for an authoritative poetics; but they have also been conscious of how their arguments proceed in a way contrary to their origins in a moment of competing styles, and aware that poetic devices are as regrettable as they are necessary. Thus, in an admiration for Pope, which is always implicit satire upon post-Romantic writing, our modern Augustans are conscious historicists. In the same way, traditional rhyming after 1795 is always conscious redemption, and implies a historical judgment of the literary possibilities of a device in a given era and a specific context of meaning. But such usage is never in itself an exemption from the requirements of history. Philip Larkin's impeccable stanzas may appear to spring from a previous century but, in fact, date themselves by their technique of relating the sentences to the rhyming, and of building a quatrain out of two couplets:

> I listen to money singing. It's like looking down
> From long French windows at a provincial town,
> The slums, the canal, the churches ornate and mad
> In the evening sun. It is intensely sad.[50]

The passage consists of three sentences: the first and third are brief, but the one in the middle, which includes three of the four rhyme words at line ends, is descriptive, accumulative, stretching into every line of the quatrain, taking up the whole (nonrhyming) middle two lines, providing thereby a way to bracket lines as against rhymes, sentences against lines, lines against themselves. The effect, terribly symmetrical, is of box within box. Immaculate: but even here one watches sheer syntax justify the otherwise arbitrary yoking of two detachable couplets into a four line stanza. It is no trick, but rather the success of skill which redeems and re-creates the couplet by reforming and re-batching and, in this case, lengthening it into hexameters.

Though there is no reason to imagine that rhyme is disappearing, or being somehow besmirched by tactics of deformation when used by Larkin rather than Pope, it is characteristic of one sort of argument to claim that this is so. Then it becomes possible to make an explicit declaration of the exquisite superiority of rhyme. In fact, this is the bias presented in that compendious and useful book, Henry Lanz's *The Physical Basis of Rime*, and in the witty defenses of rhyme written by Samuel Daniel (1603) and by Donald Davie (1970). The last of these, being jauntily rhymed on the model of Butler's *Hudibras*, is all the more winning as an argument that "what was built as Liberty Hall / Allows few liberties at all."[51] Davie's statement is judgmental, even Augustan in its assumption that rhyme in satire is the emblem of the writer's adequacy to pronounce. And yet in many other recent poems, indeed in many poems by Donald Davie, surface plausibility and hard closure are not seen as ultimate virtues. In an age like the present, which distrusts teleological effects, rhyme, as affording the ring of authority and conclusiveness, will be felt inappropriate; other, less emphatic types of rhyme will be revived or invented.

To convey sincerity in art sentences, post-Romantic writing finds itself in the curious position of planning out elaborate effects of unpredictability and hesitation. One tactic, far less common or interesting than imagined by the defenders of rhyme, is the antiteleological abandonment of the device. Robert Bridges, who may be taken as representing a crisis of versification in the period after Tennyson and before Pound and Eliot, said in 1912: "Anyone may see that serious rhyme is now exhausted in English verse."[52] Though this proved false, such statements have increased in number if not subtlety since Bridges, and very likely are the provocation to defenders of the device. Far more sophisticated is the frequent assertion, formulated here by E. E. Cummings, that only certain rhymes, "like Gillette Razor Blades / having been used and reused / to the mystical moment of dulness, emphatically are / Not To Be Resharpened."[53] T. S. Eliot felt that the freeing of rhymes from line-end position would tend to drive out bad usage; and W. C. Williams independently said the same—adding, as Eliot never could, that in the same way true measure would develop only when meter was surpassed.[54] After 1910 the writing of Eliot, Williams, Pound, and other modernists tended to make intensely problematic all received accounts of the device, accounts typified by

George Saintsbury's statement of that year in an appendix on rhyme in his vast *History of English Prosody*: "On the whole, rhyme should come at the end of something."[55] There is not now a deflation of rhyme like Pushkin's "snows-rose" gag; there is simple omission, or, far more fascinating, an extension of the meaning of "rhyme" and of "the end of something." This has happened altogether quietly, but I believe it now has the dimensions of a major stylistic innovation.

Every encounter with a blank space in the table of forms increases the chances of rhyme. That phrase has its origins in Charles Baudelaire, the poet, as Walter Benjamin presents him, of the modern city in the era of high capitalism. Baudelaire, says Benjamin, wrests his poetic booty from the phantom crowd of words, conveying the experience of mass industrial society, of city shock, in his subject itself and in his prosody. In a poem, Baudelaire speaks of making his way through words with a fencer's feints, a fencer's stabbing prosody:

> Je vais m'exercer seul a ma fantasque escrime,
> Flairant dans tous les coins *les hasards de la rime*,
> Trébuchant sur les mots comme sur les pavés,
> Heurtant parfois des vers depuis longtemps rêvés.[56]

So extreme is this situation that the survival of lyric poetry is put into question. It will, apparently, sustain itself by an appropriate technique that announces, in every smallest deflection of grammar, sound, and punctuation, with W. C. Williams, "This rhetoric is real!" In practice this would mean emphasizing the eventfulness of speech acts, translating the experience of shock to prosody, displaying the fortuitousness of aesthetic experience as much as the orderliness. Here rhyme would come as a lucky stumble, a foreseen surprise even upon rereading. Rhyme is cognitively repeatable as chance since language is linear and must be re-encoded in sequence. In art speech where there is sequence there will be surprise, though not the surprise of reminiscence, which is repetition directed backward, mere memory. Literary equivalences elicit rather the form of repetition Kierkegaard defined as remembrance carried in advance, such that we meet ourselves and our language habits at every turn slightly estranged and renewed.

And thus Charles Tomlinson writes a whole poem that explicates a passing phrase of Baudelaire, "The Chances of Rhyme":

> The chances of rhyme are like the chances of meeting—
>   In the finding fortuitous, but once found, binding:
> They say, they signify and they succeed, where to succeed
>   Means not success, but a way forward
> If unmapped, a literal, not a royal succession;
>   Though royal (it may be) is the adjective or region
> That we, nature's royalty, are led into.
>   Yes. We are led, though we seem to lead
> Through a fair forest, an Arden (a rhyme
>   For Eden)—breeding ground for beasts
> Not bestial, but loyal and legendary, which is more
>   Than nature's are. Yet why should we speak
> Of art, of life, as if the one were all form
>   And the other all Sturm-und-Drang? And I think
> Too, we should confine to Crewe or to Mow
>   Cop, all those who confuse the fortuitousness
> Of art with something to be met with only
>   At extremity's brink, reducing thus
> Rhyme to a kind of rope's end, a glimpsed grass
>   To be snatched at as we plunge past it—
> Nostalgic, after all, for a hope deferred.
>   To take chances, as to make rhymes
> Is human, but between chance and impenitence
>   (A half-rhyme) come dance, vigilance
> And circumstance (meaning all that is there
>   Besides you, when you are there). And between
> Rest-in-Peace and precipice,
>   Inertia and perversion, come the varieties

> Increase, lease, re-lease (in both
>   Senses); and immersion, conversion—of inert
> Mass, that is, into energies to combat confusion.
>   Let rhyme be my conclusion.[57]

The poem comprises everything of importance I have said about device and modernity. If we consider that rhyme stands for the whole being of poetry, if we look for rhyme as the "rope's end" of each line, we shall reduce lyric poetry to its prominent devices and verbal icons. If we inflate the importance of the device we are more likely to see it lost than if we understand its historical and prosodic-cognitive function in detail and with the proper suspicion. With its lighter cargo, lyric poetry may still flourish if we use rhyme sparingly, forcing semantic connections, invoking the energies of language as well as the "Rest-in-Peace" of convention. We need to understand verbal art as process as well as product, as speech act as well as objective fact: neither "all form" nor all feeling, but a structure of relations, a formal-semantic entanglement.

In their profound linkages, our words are us. But some words (as James Schuyler says) "are briefly worse than others," and these "The Chances of Rhyme" will ask us to transform. At the end of Charles Tomlinson's poem, in a dazzling disply of word chaining, he speaks of the mind's conversion of the inert mass of language, by means of rhyme, "into energies to combat confusion." Thus can a single device, in its tiny but crucial instance, testify to the economy of the human intelligence and its ability to make meaning.

Conclusion

I have advanced the following hypotheses: (1) that since the history of poetic forms taken by themselves would tend to distort the delicate interrelation of writer, work, and society, it is necessary to find principles of coherence beyond the postulate of technical innovation—it is necessary to outline a theory of structural historicism; (2) that to take the shift from Neoclassicism to Romanticism in 1795 in the strong sense helps us to understand essential aspects in the relation of literary modernity to the other modernity of bourgeois civilization; (3) that under historical conditions of modernity, poetry and commentators alike are enmeshed in a contradictory structure of thought where the highest twin values are the corporeality and the transparency of the medium of language; (4) that the question of literariness or marked language is a subset of the apparent contradiction between modernity and history—from looking at literature through the concept of modernity as it is related to history, we can understand more clearly than before the distinctive nature of literature; (5) that we can also understand better what literature is if we trace the differences between literary language and natural language, as well as the difference between literary language and "failed" literature, children's writing, and folk writing, all of which employ many of the same cognitive structures as literature proper; and (6) that in the ways it is distorted, employed directly, or significantly omitted, rhyme is the representative of all structural devices in the modern period.

All six hypotheses were derived from a hypothesis that, as soon as stated, began to seem radically insufficient. I began with the notion that innovative ideas of the poem, notably free verse and the prose poem, had tended largely to discredit rhyming poetry in English, making rhyme too sweet and expected for the writers most conscious of the historical situation of their art. I couldn't prove my thesis, either in theory or by any form of statistical evaluation. Nor could I prove it by interpreting single texts. But I could easily find arguments against my thesis in some of the innovations that have appeared in rhyme, as it is employed by traditional poets as well as by those who have written in the free verse tradition. I came to realize that rhyme was more resilient and various than I had imagined earlier. I finally came to realize that my task was to explain how historical events themselves have caused rhyme to be changed, or to be abandoned and replaced by other forms. At this point, my study took on a more general direction: as an experiment, I determined to discover what I could about the relationship of device and modernity, when the two concepts were considered simultaneously.

For bringing these two concepts together in this way, I began to realize the relevance of some of the ideas of W. Jackson Bate and Harold Bloom, particularly theories they proposed about the English poet and the burden of the past he must abide.[1] One outcome I hoped to achieve was to suport their accounts of literary influence in the strong sense as institution, or as repression. "That which is creative must create itself": Keats's warning to himself can only remind us, too, of the embarrassment of our literary lateness and dependence. With such imperatives does the Romantic and post-Romantic intelligence define itself. The need to be unprecedented, self-created, self-sustaining, contradicts or seems to contradict our absolute knowledge that we are latecomers who owe debts, intellectual and moral.

The Chances of Rhyme has drawn out only what seemed exciting from the unwieldy matrix of unsystematic scholarship on the subject. All I claim to have done in this essay is to have refined the problem. I could not hope to solve it completely. The conduct of the argument depends to a large extent upon examples selected from many others as testimony, and upon the handling of those representative examples: quotation of complete poems, usually, and detailed analysis from part to the movement of the whole formal utterance. My aim has been, so far as possible, to re-position rhyme in our interpretation of line and poem, and to re-position the poem in our interpretation of history.

Commentators, not poets, have removed devices both from the poetic line and from history. The New Critics, I have said, went too far in the direction of reifying rhyme and other devices. To correct their emphasis, I have revived the once despised concept of organic form. I have argued that the leading idea of Romantic and post-Romantic style is the concept of cooperative behavior, taken first in the sense of the poem's internal unity, the coherence of the act of mind (author's; reader's) it notates, and also in the sense that this unity persuades, implicates, indeed constitutes a reader, who works within the poem by imagining its rhetoric as personal speech.

Inevitably, taking this line has involved questioning certain premises. I have suggested that only by accepting the autonomy and object quality of the text is the New Criticism able to purchase the exclusion of other aspects of the theory of organic form—aspects closer to the center of the Romantic paradigm because they reveal more and more subtle relationships. New Critical speculation is put into conflict with itself, a contradiction Paul de Man has called "flagrant": "On the one hand, we blame American criticism for considering literary texts as if they were natural objects but, on the other hand, we praise it for possessing a sense of formal unity that belongs precisely to a living and natural organism. . . . The introduction of intentionality would imperil the organic analogy and lead to the loss of the sense of form; hence the understandable need of the New Critics to protect their greatest source of strength."[2] Very likely, New Critical disapproval of Romanticism and avant-garde prosodies comes, at least in part, from a belief that organicist poetics in its other, more primordial phase obliterates genre, poetic pattern, and also the creative freedom of the poet. The idea of the poem-as-organism has been called "only a metaphor" and a misleading one (Graham Hough), a determinism that makes of the artist almost a mechanical agent (Pater in his essay titled "Coleridge"), a trick to preclude the anxiety of influence (Bloom), the mere restatement of Aristotelian premises (Hough; Wimsatt), and largely a way of assuming "a psychologistic conception of meaning which mistakenly identifies meaning with mental processes rather than with the object of those processes."[3] These arguments seem less crushing, however, if we consider the organic analogy as the essential expression of a resolvable dilemma in logic, namely as the manifesto statement of a limiting case. Typically, Graham Hough is deceived by avant-garde hyperbole, and caught in its frame of reference, when he reacts against organicism by demanding what might be the real distinction between organic and mechanical form: "How are we to determine whether the form of a work of literature has been externally imposed or is co-natural with its conception? There does not seem to be any way of doing this."[4] Indeed there is not. The appropriate question would ask what devices a work employs to achieve a relative transparence, or seeming spontaneity of rhetoric: how a voice is entangled in the words, and by what means modernity makes apparently open structures out of essentially closed ones.

We need not lose our sense of form if we take into account the historical necessity of organicist overstatement and then proceed to identify and interpret successful instances of non-traditional poetic patterning.[5] How might we go beyond the tendency of New Criticism to reify the text as object, its tendency to forget that the work is made up of symbols as well as signs? An alternative poetics would, by contrast, understand poetry as a special rapport of language to the world, and of language to language. This rapport, following Henri Meschonnic, we may call *the intention of poetry*, wherein the work is "object and subject, closed as system, [and yet] open into the interior of itself as creativity and to the outside as reading."[6] Such an interpretive practice would resist the urge of some theories to make the whole poem disappear into its numerous internal connections. The only responsible method of creating a historical poetics would seem to be a method that preserves all those internal rapports, and traces, in turn, their affiliations to the worlds of reference, the reader, and history. New Criticism's neglect of those worlds, and its attacks on expressive theory from Longinus to the present, would have to be met with a demonstration that accounts of the poem as creativity and as reading do in fact see something that is really there in the work, and something that is otherwise missed.[7] Seeing the work in history, and history inscribed in the work, one comes to see the work's own conditions of possibility, and thus to date and read it. More precisely, one comes to see more clearly how one is able to read it—what kind of structural and historical competences are involved.

We attain a strong reading only when we have seen the poem's conventions not as laws of nature but as historical occurrences, for then we have freed structural analysis from the myth of structure. The myth of structure persists into the post-New Critical period as a definition of literary constructs: measure as versification, not as prosody; literary language as lexis, not as syntax; interpretation as an account of the components of a product, not of the conditions of a practice.

Attempting as it does to reverse these priorities, structural historicism sees in the poem what was always there; it sees the same thing the New Criticism saw, but draws back and focuses the lens to take in the social and psychological context of the work's moment and the reader's moment.

The structural historicism I am outlining is based on the assumption that creation and appreciation of verbal art is a practice that comes to know itself, which takes itself as its own object. The poem has no "use," in the way we customarily know that we can use a piece of equipment to plow a field, to dig an excavation, or level a slope. It has no "value" in exchange for some other object we need or desire. We cannot trade a poem for food, clothing, or shelter, although poets have from time to time attempted to do so. No, a poem has value only as a part of life itself. Its sole purpose and result is to create or appreciate a mode of self-knowledge—for both the poet and his or her perceptive reader. As Marx W. Wartofsky has written, this activity is not merely self-reflective, but primarily transformative: "It is not the product—the artwork, the completed and dead image—which is the mirror of human nature; but rather the process of artistic creation itself; *and* the proces of *re*creation in the act of aesthetic appreciation which constitutes the active humanizing [practice] of art."[8] So actual participation in art, whether an act of creation or appreciation, is the way human nature comes to represent itself to itself, and there are concrete social reasons why this transforming activity is worthwhile. After all, if we have power over words, words have power over us.

Yet this humanizing practice becomes difficult if the artwork is taken as an autonomous and independent reality. We need, in fact, to break from the notion of isolating the object, because in literature and in nearly all the other arts except the visual arts, as Raymond Williams has written,

what we have are not objects but *notations*. These notations have to be interpreted in an active way, according to particular conventions.

. . . The relationship between the making of a work of art and the reception of a work of art, is always active, and subject to conventions which in themselves are forms of social organization and relationship, and this is radically different from the production and consumption of an object. [Art] is indeed an activity and a practice, and in its accessible forms, although it may in some arts have the character of a material object, it is still only accessible through active perception and interpretation.[9]

Now, one of the axioms of Romantic aesthetics holds that no element of the work should be prior to or independent of the work's composition. What if we extended this axiom to the ontology of the work itself, assuming that interpretive like historical theories are hypotheses which assert that literary events, or statements about them, are not independent of other events or statements? What if we assumed that literary knowledge is historical knowledge? This "complex of extending active relationships," in Raymond Williams's words, does in fact oppose a naive confusing of literary with existential reality. Thus structural historicism affords one answer to those who would point to "the difficulty of deciding between literary symbolism and the symbolism which is all language."[10] The practice of art does constitute human reality only through symbols. However, among those symbols, literature is differently constitutive by seeking to preserve and exaggerate the ambiguity of text and speech. Especially after 1795, the compositional process occurs in and through symbols that try to look like signs, in and through technique as sincerity and rhetoric as voice. The attempt to override the discriminations, always destined to fail and yet always the urging behind the work's innovative qualities, is premised on the discriminations themselves.

Notes

PREFACE

1. The term is Northrop Frye's in *T. S. Eliot* (New York: Capricorn Books, 1972), p. 28. Since the seventeenth century, *rhyme* has been the more common spelling—an absurdity that came about when scholars attempted to derive the device from the Greek *rhythmos* (whence *rhythm* comes). The present study adopts this by now conventional usage in preference to the older *rime*, because one of its interests lies in the relation of rhyme to meter in the rhythmic construction of the poetic line. To my eye, also, the learned spelling rhyme is more acceptably familiar than the original rime.

2. Robert Creeley, "Was That a Real Poem or Did You Just Make It Up Yourself?" in *American Poets in 1976*, ed. William Heyen (Indianapolis: Bobbs-Merrill Company, Inc., 1976), pp. 50–51.

3. Thomas Campion's *Observations in the Art of English Poesie* dates 1602; a year later Samuel Daniel's *Defense of Ryme* responded in statements quite similar to Creeley's. E.g., "for sure in an eminent spirit whome Nature hath fitted for that mysterie, Ryme is no impediment to [the poet's] conceit, but rather gives him wings to mount and carries him, not out of his course, but as it were beyond his power to a farre happier flight." *A Defense of Rime* (London, 1603); reprint ed., A. C. Sprague, ed., Chicago: University of Chicago Press, 1965), pp. 137–138.

4. Parker Tyler, Preface to Charles Henri Ford, ed., *A Little Anthology of the Poem in Prose*, in *New Directions Fourteen* (1953; republished by Kraus Reprint Corporation, New York, 1967), p. 336.

141

1: Historical and Structural Coordinates

1. Historical and psychological aspects of the ideal of sincerity since Romanticism are discussed in David Perkins, *Wordsworth and the Poetry of Sincerity* (Cambridge, Mass.: Harvard University Press, 1964); and in Lionel Trilling, *Sincerity and Authenticity* (Cambridge, Mass.: Harvard University Press, 1973).

2. The fuller context of Jakobson's sentence may be useful: "The selection is produced on the base of equivalence, similarity and dissimilarity, synonymity and antonymity, while the combination, the build up of the sequence, is based on contiguity. *The poetic function projects the principle of equivalence from the axis of selection into the axis of combination.* Equivalence is promoted to the constitutive device of the sequence. In poetry one syllable is equalized with any other syllable of the same sequence; word stress is assumed to equal word stress, as unstress equals unstress; prosodic long is matched with long, and short with short; word boundary equals word boundary, no boundary equals no boundary; syntactic pause equals no pause. Syllables are converted into units of measure, and so are morae or stresses." The passage may be found in Roman Jakobson, "Closing Statement: Linguistics and Poetics," in *Style in Language,* ed. Thomas A. Sebeok (Cambridge, Mass.: M.I.T. Press, 1960), p. 358. Elsewhere Jakobson writes that "equivalence in difference is the cardinal problem of language and the pivotal concern of linguistics": "On Linguistic Aspects of Translation," *Selected Writings* (The Hague: Mouton 1971), II, 262.

3. Since *homoeoteleuton* is a term that returns in the next chapter, in a context of debate, it is well at the outset to affiliate my definition with that given in *The Princeton Encyclopedia of Poetry and Poetics,* ed. Alex Preminger (Princeton, N.J.: Princeton University Press, 1965), p. 353: "it describes similar case-endings in proximity, whether in prose or verse, e.g., in Naevius' Saturnian: 'bicorpores Gigantes / / magnique Atlantes.' When homoeoteleuton of more than one syllable occurs at the end of two or more lines in succession, it becomes rhyme. . . . It is generally agreed that homoeoteleuton and rhyme in quantitative meters were intentional, whether the effect was similar or not to that achieved by their use in the accentual verse of later Latin and of modern languages."

4. Notions of periodization in the previous paragraphs follow Renato Poggioli, *The Theory of the Avant-Garde,* trans. Gerald Fitzgerald (Cambridge, Mass.: Harvard University Press, 1968). I date

the birth of this paradigm at 1795, the year of Coleridge's experiment in the new mode, "Eolian Harp," and also the year of Wordsworth's recension of *Descriptive Sketches*, a poem that (in couplets) struggles against the whole style and ethos of the Augustan heroic couplet. Shortly thereafter follows Coleridge's "Christabel," an influential fragment in accentual measures which subverts the quantitative analogies on which Augustan form was based; *Lyrical Ballads* in 1798 as the first book in the new way of writing; and the manifesto of the new style in Wordsworth's 1800 Preface. The year 1795 is chosen for this break in Fredic Pottle's "Synchrony and Diachrony: A Plea for the Use in Literary Studies of Saussure's Concepts and Terminology," in *Literary Theory and Structure*, ed. Frank Brady, John Palmer, and Martin Price (New Haven: Yale University Press, 1973).

5. Matei Calinescu, *Faces of Modernity: Avant-Garde, Decadence, Kitsch* (Bloomington and London: Indiana University Press, 1977); the quotation on aesthetic modernity comes from p. 10. Also very useful on the subject of modernity is Herbert N. Schneidau's *Sacred Discontent: The Bible and Western Tradition* (Baton Rouge: Lousiana State University Press, 1976), esp. Chapter V.

6. Paul de Man, "Literary History and Literary Modernity," in his *Blindness and Insight: Essays in the Rhetoric of Contemporary Criticism* (New York: Oxford University Press, 1971), p. 162; ibid., pp. 161, 164.

7. David Craig, "Towards Laws of Literary Development," in David Craig, ed., *Marxists on Literature: An Anthology* (Harmondsworth, Middlesex: Penguin, 1975), p. 160.

8. W. K. Wimsatt, *Literary Criticism: A Short History* (New York: Knopf, 1966), p. 399.

9. W. Jackson Bate, *Prefaces to Criticism* (Garden City, N.Y.: Doubleday, 1959), pp. 116–117.

10. Ibid., pp. 115–116.

11. Earl Wasserman, *The Subtler Language* (Baltimore: The Johns Hopkins Press, 1959), p. 11.

12. S. T. Coleridge, "On Poesy or Art," *Biographia Literaria*, ed. J. Shawcross (London: Oxford University Press, 1907), II, 258.

13. *The Prose Works of William Wordsworth*, ed. W. J. B. Owen and Jane Worthington Smyser (Oxford: Oxford University Press, 1974), I, 161.

14. Ibid., III, 77.

15. Charles Olson, *Selected Writings*, ed. Robert Creeley (New York: New Directions, 1966), pp. 17, 44.

16. Coleridge, "On Poesy or Art," p. 262.

17. Ibid., pp. 254–255.

18. S. T. Coleridge, *Shakespearean Criticism*, ed. T. M. Raysor (London: J. M. Dent & Sons, Ltd., 1960), I, 198.

19. B. J. Pendlebury, *The Art of the Rhyme* (New York: Scribners, 1971), p. 10.

20. I refer to Viktor Zhirmunski, *Rifma, ee istorija i teorija* [Rhyme: Its History and Theory] (Petersburg: Academia, 1923); and Thomas Eekman, *The Realm of Rime: A Study of Rime in the Poetry of the Slavs* (Amsterdam: Hakkert, 1974). Other twentieth-century books devoted to rhyme are Charles F. Richardson, A Study of English Rhyme (Hanover, N.H.: Printed for Classroom Use, 1909); Henry Lanz, *The Physical Basis of Rime: An Essay on the Aesthetics of Sound* (Stanford: Stanford University Press, 1931; reprinted., New York: Greenwood Press, 1968); and B. J. Pendlebury (See n. 19).

21. Lanz, *The Physical Basis of Rime.*

22. W. K. Wimsatt, "One Relation of Rhyme to Reason"; collected in *The Verbal Icon: Studies in the Meaning of Poetry* (Lexington: University of Kentucky Press, 1954), pp. 152–166.

23. Ibid., p. 156.

24. W. K. Wimsatt, "Rhetoric and Poems: The Example of Swift," delivered at the Modern Language Association Convention in New York City, December 1974; quoted from a typescript copy loaned by the author, and used by permission of Mrs. William Kurtz Wimsatt.

25. Wimsatt, "One Relation of Rhyme to Reason," p. 160.

26. Ibid., p. 163.

27. Thanks are due to Mrs. William Kurtz Wimsatt for permission to use this portion of a letter by the late Professor Wimsatt.

28. This sentence refers respectively to Henry Lanz, *The Physical Basis of Rime*, and to Alastair Fowler, "The Selection of Literary Constructs," *New Literary History* 7, 1 (Autumn 1975), esp. 42, 53.

29. Josephine Miles, *Poetry and Change* (Berkeley, Los Angeles, London: University of California Press, 1974), p. 21.

30. Edward Stankiewicz, "Poetic and Non-Poetic Language," *Poetics-Poetyka-Poetika I*, ed. Donald Davie et al. (Warsaw: Mouton with Polish Scientific Publishers, 1961), p. 16.

31. Viktor Zhirmunski, quoted by Edgar Lohner, "The Intrinsic Method: Some Reconsiderations," in *The Disciplines of Criticism*, ed. Peter Demetz, Thomas Greene, and Lowry Nelson, Jr. (New

Haven and London: Yale University Press, 1968), p. 157. Zhirmunski was not one of the formalists, but his phrasing gives the essence
of their position.

32. Boris Ejxenbaum, quoted by Lohner, ibid., pp. 158–159.

33. Zhirmunski's work is reassessed and brilliantly extended by
Michael Shapiro, *Asymmetry: An Inquiry into the Linguistic Structure of Poetry* (Amsterdam: North-Holland, 1976); fourth and final
chapter, on rhyme, has been published as "Sémiotique de la rime,"
Poétique 20 (1974), 501–519.

34. Summary statement on formalism by Edgar Lohner, "The
Instrinsic Method," p. 159.

35. Roman Jakobson, "Co je poesie?" *Volny Smery* XXX
(1933–1934), 229–239; from an unpublished translation by Leon
Burnett.

36. True, in the mid-1920s before their dispersal due to political
pressure, the formalists produced a few statements on literary
history as evolution: the theses of Tynjanov and Jakobson, depending on categories fruitfully adopted from linguistics, show how diachrony may be a relation between successive systems (Tynjanov and
Jakobson, "The Problems of Literary Studies and Linguistics,"
[1928]). Again, arguing historically, the formalists do indicate how
the long-range effect of the laying bare of devices is a demonstration
that a previous canonic usage is not irrevocable. They knew that in
different historical periods the same literary device could change its
weighting and whole rationale. Tynjanov knew that in certain
periods a careful anachronism is the most extreme form of innovation. And yet in their brief flourishing there was not time for these
scholars, trained before the revolution, fully to historicize themselves. Fredric Jameson has written of the formalists with mixed sym-
pathy for their constitutive discoveries and terminologies and disapproval of their lack, *au fond*, of a historical sense; see *The Prison-
House of Language: A Critical Account of Structuralism and Russian
Formalism* (Princeton, N.J.: Princeton University Press, 1972).

37. Victor Erlich, *Russian Formalism: History-Doctrine*, 2d ed.
(The Hague-Paris: Mouton, 1965), esp. Chapter XV, "Stock-
Taking."

38. *Letters From Joseph Conrad 1895–1924*, edited with introduction and notes by Edward Garnett (Indianapolis, Indiana: Bobbs-
Merrill, 1928) p. 135.

39. O. M. Brik, "Contributions to the Study of Verse Language,"
in *Readings in Russian Poetics: Formalist and Structuralist Views*,

ed. Ladislav Matejka and Krystyna Pomorska (Cambridge, Mass.: M.I.T. Press, 1971), p. 125.

40. See Dwight L. Bollinger, "Rime, Assonance, and Morpheme Analysis," *Word* 6, no. 2 (August 1950), 130.

41. Jakobson, "Closing Statement: Linguistics and Poetics."

42. *Rhyming Cockney Slang,* ed. Jack Jones (Bristol, 1971).

43. "Dad's Army," a BBC Production.

44. Shapiro, *Asymmetry,* both quotations pp. 142–143.

45. *The Poetry of Robert Frost,* ed. Robert Connery Lathem (New York: Holt, Rinehart and Winston, 1969).

46. "Poetry and Verse," *The Journals and Papers of Gerard Manley Hopkins,* ed. Humphrey House (London: Oxford University Press, 1959), p. 289.

47. Wimsatt, "One Relation of Rhyme to Reason," p. 155.

48. For an excellent study of "some constants in the language of lyric poetry, some fundamental forms underlying the figures of imagery and the movements of sound and rhythm" (p. vii), see Andrew Welsh, *Roots of Lyric: Primitive Poetry and Modern Poetics* (Princeton, N.J.: Princeton University Press, 1978).

49. Two twentieth-century schools of poetry have avoided rhyme on principle: the deep-image or surrealist school from Trakl and Neruda, Lorca and Vallejo, down to American poets like Robert Bly and W. S. Merwin; and New York School poets including Frank O'Hara and John Ashbery. The former poets rely on the image as the central vehicle of persuasion; the latter rely on pseudonarrative, zaniness with language, and direct statement. (For an instance of the latter school, see the playful hyperbole of O'Hara's "Personism: A Manifesto": "I don't believe in god, so I don't have to make elaborately sounded structures," in *The Selected Poems of Frank O'Hara,* ed. Donald Allen [New York: Vintage Books, 1974], p. xiii.) These poets can be magnificent, but their disparagement of rhyme as an act of self-conscious virtuosity, their reliance on substitutive innovations with image and statement, are not evidence for a decline of rhyme in the twentieth century. Quite the contrary. The argument in chapter one has already accounted for their practice by speaking of the salient omission of rhyme. Under historical conditions of modernity, unrhyme has always the character of a guerrilla war against (and presupposing) rhyme. In such an era, successful rhymelessness in one sector of professional poetry always signifies rhyme's valid presence in another sector.

2: Device: Aspects of History and Structure

1. "Our need mocks our gear" is a phrase from Adrienne Rich's "Double Monologue," *Snapshots of a Daughter-In-Law: Poems, 1954–1962* (New York: W. W. Norton, 1967), p. 34.

2. *Letters of Wallace Stevens,* ed. Holly Stevens (New York: Knopf, 1966), p. 157. The letter dates August 19, 1909.

3. Mayakovsky, "A Conversation with the Inspector of Taxes About Poetry," *Mayakovsky,* trans. and ed. Herbert Marshall (New York: Hill and Wang, 1965), p. 353.

4. T. S. Eliot, "Reflections on Vers Libre," *New Statesman,* March 3, 1917, p. 519; reprinted in *To Criticize the Critic* (New York: Farrar, Straus & Giroux, 1965).

5. For example, Henry Lanz, *The Physical Basis of Rime: An Essay on the Aesthetics of Sound* (Stanford: Stanford University Press, 1931); Martin Dodsworth's introduction to *The Survival of Poetry: A Contemporary Survey,* ed. Dodsworth (London: Faber and Faber, 1970), pp. 11–36; and Kingsley Amis's introduction to *The New Oxford Book of English Light Verse,* chosen and edited by Kingsley Amis (New York: Oxford University Press, 1978), esp. pp. xxi–xxii.

6. Charles Tomlinson, *The Way of a World* (Oxford: Oxford University Press, 1969), p. 59.

7. J. S. Schütze, *Versuch einer Theorie des Reimes nach Inhalt und Form* (1802); discussed in Lanz, *Physical Basis of Rhyme,* pp. 161–167, esp. p. 166 for the definition here given. My phrasing, of course, neglects the practice (admired in Middle English and Old French) of "rich" rhyme, or rhyming on homonyms: two sounds and two meanings in one spelling.

8. Tomlinson's phrase is from "The Chances of Rhyme" (see n. 6); relevant studies by the linguist, Dwight L. Bollinger, and the three mentioned scholars are listed in the Selected Bibliography.

9. See Selected Bibliography for details.

10. Patrick Condon, my research assistant at the University of California, San Diego, for two months at an early stage of this essay, wrote to me in a letter: "For the fact of rhyme lends itself to particular categories of interpretation. Rhyme is, historically, manipulated as an intentional image. It is artifact, and image of its users: this both consciously and unconsciously. Consciously, rhyme is made a fighting issue between conflicting poetics and the ideologies they

represent. Unconsciously an orientation toward rhyme as well as its particular employment manifest a structure of perception and self-perception: not necessarily in agreement with explicit statements." This ideal of a sociology of literary form has helped focus the present inquiry.

11. There remains the possibility that these words were pronounced alike in Shakespeare's day. Henry Cecil Wyld, in *English Rhyme from Surrey to Pope* (London, 1923; reprinted, New York: Russell & Russell, 1965) argues that rhymes reflect the actual speech of a period and that we may deduce an earlier period's pronunciation from its literary rhymes. Pope's "tea" is pronounced "tay," in order to rhyme with "obey." But if a variety of conventional deformations are permissible in any period, as a way of extending the range of homophones, then Wyld's thesis is faulty.

12. Vladimir Nabokov, *Notes on Prosody*, from the commentary to his translation of Pushkin's *Eugene Onegin* (New York: Pantheon Books, 1964), p. 82: "Rhyme is not a component of meter, not part of the final foot, but rather its stub or its shoe, or its spur." A similar ornamentalist view of the device, to which the present essay takes exception by showing rhyme's implication in the line, may be seen in the generative metrics of Morris Halle and S. J. Keyser, "Chaucer and the Study of Prosody," *College English* 28 (December 1966), pp. 187–219.

13. Perhaps the best beginnings at a notation are to be found in two articles by David I. Masson, "Vowel and Consonant Patterns in Poetry," *Journal of Aesthetics and Art Criticism* 12 (1953–1954), 213–227; "Sound-Repetition Terms," *Poetics-Poetika-Poetyka* I (Warsaw: Mouton and Polish Scientific Publishers, 1961), 189–199. Also valuable is chapter 6, "Patterns of Sound," in Geoffrey N. Leech, *A Linguistic Guide to English Poetry* (London: Longmans, 1969).

14. Harold Whitehall, "From Linguistics to Poetry," in *Sound and Poetry*, ed. with an introduction by Northrop Frye (New York: Columbia University Press, 1957), p. 139.

15. G. S. Fraser in *Metre, Rhyme and Free Verse* (London: Methuen, 1970), p. 59, writes: "Rhyme, compared to rhythm, is a simple topic. . . ."

16. Whitehall, "From Linguistics to Poetry," p. 139. John W. Draper finds "The Origin of Rhyme" in Chinese folk-poetry of the *Shih Ching*; see his essay in *Revue de la littérature comparée*, 3 (1957), esp. 83–86. A more recent study of "repetitions of sound in

parallel metrical positions" finds that rhyme in classical Latin poetry is not an unintentional side effect but a conscious device, clearly described in the ancient literary theory of sound pattern and rhetorical figures: evidence that challenges the claim for vernacular invention of rhyming poetry. See Eva H. Guggenheimer, *Rhyme Effects and Rhyming Figures* (The Hague-Paris: Mouton, 1972).

17. William Beare, *Latin Verse and European Song* (London: Methuen, 1957), p. 255.

18. Ibid., p. 256.

19. March, *Latin Hymns*, quoted by Richardson, *Study of English Rhyme*, p. 22.

20. In this and the next quotation, Beare summarizes Lote's point from the latter's *Histoire du vers français* (1949); see Beare, *Latin Verse and European Song*, p. 256.

21. The definitive account of "The English Tail-Rhyme Romances," by A. McI. Trounce, may be found in four consecutive issues of *Medium Aevum*, beginning with Vol. I, no. 1 (May 1932).

22. Lanz, *The Physical Basis of Rime*, p. 53.

23. I have quoted all but the first two lines of Part I, stanza 7, *Sir Gawain and the Green Knight*, ed. J. R. R. Tolkien and E. V. Gordon, 2d ed. ref. by Norman Davis (Oxford: Oxford University Press, 1967), pp. 4–5.

24. A fine account of Skelton's rhythms and rhymes may be found in Andrew Welsh, *Roots of Lyric: Primitive Poetry and Modern Poetics* (Princeton, N.J.: Princeton University Press, 1978), Chapter VIII.

25. "Add to that the music of the phrase, as with a Campion, to be chosen and protected"; W. C. Williams in a "final note" on Zukofsky in Louis Zukofsky, *"A" 1–12* (Ashland, Mass.: Origin Press, 1959); and see especially Williams's remarks on Campion and measure in *Spectrum* (1959).

26. *Ben Jonson*, ed. C. H. Herford and Percy and Evelyn Simpson (Oxford: Oxford University Press, 1947), 8:184.

27. In a book of major importance, Mary Ellen Rickey has shown that Crashaw "wrote, to an unusual degree, with the end of the line particularly in mind, aiming the line" toward rhymes selected from an "extremely personal" vocabulary; see Rickey, *Rhyme and Meaning in Richard Crashaw* (Lexington: University of Kentucky Press, 1961).

28. W. C. Williams, "The Pink Church," *Collected Later Poems* (New York: New Directions, 1950), p. 162.

29. Seymour Chatman has demonstrated this fact in detailed comparison of couplets by Donne and Pope, "Comparing Metrical Styles," *Style in Language*, ed. Thomas A. Sebeok (Cambridge: M.I.T. Press, 1960).

30. This is to extend Wimsatt's description of "The Augustan Mode in English Poetry": "This couplet poetry might look like a surrender to prevailing norms of clarity, distinctness, sweet reasonableness, science, and the order of nature. It was actually a polite evasion of all that. One might have thought it curious, on the face of the matter, that the great age of classical order should be at ease only in the Gothic and mystical shackles of rhyme." Wimsatt, *Hateful Contraries:* Studies in Literature and Criticism (Lexington: University of Kentucky Press, 1965), p. 152.

31. For the definitive study of closure, which this sentence summarizes, see Barbara H. Smith, *Poetic Closure: A Study of How Poems End* (Chicago: University of Chicago Press, 1968).

32. Roland Barthes, *Elements of Semiology*, trans. A. Lavers and C. Smith (London: Cape, 1967(, p. 86.

33. W. J. Ong, "A Dialectic of Aural and Objective Correlatives," in *The Barbarian Within* (New York: Macmillan, 1962), p. 29.

34. Roman Jakobson, "Closing Statement: Linguistics and Poetics," in *Style in Language*, ed. Thomas A. Sebeok (Cambridge: M.I.T. Press, 1960), p. 367.

35. Hegel writes with penetration on rhyme and prosody in *Philosophy of Fine Art*, trans. F. P. B. Osmaston (London: G. Bell and Sons, Ltd., 1920), 4: esp. 84–98.

36. Quoted, for reasons that will soon be obvious, from the version given by Henry Lanz in *The Physical Basis of Rime*, p. 172.

37. Ibid., p. 172.

38. Sigurd Burckhardt, "The Poet as Fool and Priest," *ELH* 23 (1956), p. 279. Reprinted as Chapter II of his *Shakespearean Meanings* (Princeton: Princeton University Press, 1968).

39. W. K. Wimsatt, "One Relation of Rhyme to Reason," in *The Verbal Icon: Studies in the Meaning of Poetry* (1944; Lexington: University of Kentucky Press, 1954), p. 153.

40. Craig La Drière, "Structure, Sound and Meaning," in *Sound and Poetry*, ed. Frye (New York: Columbia University Press, 1957), p. 108.

41. W. K. Wimsatt, "Rhetoric and Poems," in *The Verbal Icon*, p. 180.

42. Randall Jarrell, "A Well-To-Do Invalid," *The Lost World* (New York: Macmillan, 1965), pp. 21–23.

43. Stéphane Mallarmé, *Oeuvres complètes*, texte établi et annoté par H. Mondor et G. Jean-Aubry (Paris: Gallimard, 1945), pp. 466–467.

44. The above paragraph borrows terms and ideas from Roman Jakobson's definition of the poetic function; see especially "Linguistics and Poetics," p. 358.

45. Ernst Jandl, "Names," in *Concrete Poetry: An International Anthology*, ed. Stephen Bann (London: London Magazine Editions, 1967), p. 76.

46. From *English Folk-Rhymes*, collected by G. F. Northall (London, 1892; reprinted., Detroit, Mich., Singing Tree Press, 1968), p. 294.

47. Ibid., pp. 314, 285.

48. See Dwight L. Bollinger, "Rime, Assonance, and Morpheme Analysis," *Word* 6, no. 2 (August 1950), 117–136.

49. *English Folk-Rhymes*, pp. 346–347 for the remaining counting-out rhymes quoted here.

50. By Molly Williams Wesling. The assumption is large, and requires more demonstration than I can give here, but I would hazard that such ventures are especially important, for in some sense they recapitulate the whole history of poetry.

51. Geoffrey Hartman, "The Voice of the Shuttle: Language From the Point of View of Literature," in *Beyond Formalism: Literary Essays, 1958–1970* (New Haven and London: Yale University Press, 1970), esp. pp. 339, 347.

52. The phrase is from W. K. Wimsatt, "Imitation as Freedom: 1717–1798," *Day of the Leopards: Essays in Defense of Poems* (New Haven and London: Yale University Press, 1976), p. 118.

53. Quoted in Victor Erlich, *Russian Formalism: History-Doctrine* 2d ed. (The Hague-Paris: Mouton, 1965), p. 184.

54. See Victor H. Yngve, "The Depth Hypothesis," in Fred W. Householder, ed., *Syntactic Theory I* (Harmondsworth, Eng.: Penguin Books, 1972).

55. Jiři Levý, "The Meanings of Form and the Forms of Meaning," in *Poetics-Poetyka-Poetika* II (Warsaw: Mouton with Polish Scientific Publishers, 1966), 45–59; see p. 50.

56. Levý continues (ibid., p. 46): "Each of the three principles of arrangement on the physical level has its structural correlative in the

corresponding arrangement on the semantic level, since 'meaning,' too, is linear in character, if we regard it as a process, as a gradual apprehension of the sequence of semantic segments."

57. Wimsatt's premises have been reassessed by Hugh Kenner, "Pope's Reasonable Rhymes," *ELH* 41 (Spring 1974), 74–88; and by John Hollander, "Rhyme and the True Calling of Words," in *Vision and Resonance: Two Senses of Poetic Form* (New York: Oxford University Press, 1975), pp. 117–134.

58. From the opening of Canto IV, *Eugene Onegin*, in *Pushkin Threefold*, Originals with Linear and Metric Translations by Walter Arndt (New York: Dutton, 1972), p. 153.

59. Robert Graves, "A Slice of Wedding Cake," *Collected Poems* (Garden City, N.Y.: Doubleday, 1961), p. 300.

60. Details of Chinese versification in this paragraph rely on teaching materials prepared by Wai-lim Yip for his classes at the University of California, San Diego. Other valuable accounts of the subject are: James J. Y. Liu, *The Art of Chinese Poetry* (Chicago: University of Chicago Press, 1962); Roman Jakobson, "The Modular Design of Chinese Regulated Verse," in *Échanges et communications: Mélanges offerts à Claude Levi-Strauss* (The Hague-Paris: Mouton, 1970), pp. 597–605; and Hans H. Frankel, "Classical Chinese," in *Versification: Major Language Types*, ed. with a foreword by W. K. Wimsatt (New York: Modern Language Association, New York University Press, 1972). The definitive scholarly treatment is by Wang Li, *Han-yü shih-lü hsüeh* (Shanghai, 1962).

61. George A. Miller, "The Magical Number Seven, Plus or Minus Two: Some Limits on Our Capacity for Processing Information," in *The Psychology of Communication: Seven Essays* (Baltimore, Md.: Penguin Books, 1969), pp. 14–44.

62. Lanz, *The Physical Basis of Rime*, p. 235.

63. Jan M. Meijer, "Verbal Art as Interference between a Cognitive and an Aesthetic Structure," in Jan van der Eng and Mojmír Grygar, *Structure of Texts and Semiotics of Culture* (The Hague-Paris: Mouton, 1973), p. 318.

64. *New Statesman* 84, no. 2157 (July 21, 1972), 105. "When Runcorn's Gentians" is by Roy Fuller; "Pope mocked Belinda" is by Dorothy Colmer.

65. Dr. John Barrell of King's College, Cambridge, writes in a letter: "I take it the point of the Widnes-Kidneys rhyme is that in

Lancs it *is* a perfect rhyme (Widnes=Wídniz). That's why he likes northern things, or a part of the things he likes."

66. See Donald Bligh, *What's the Use of Lectures?* (Harmondsworth, Middlesex: Penguin Books, 1972), p. 56: "When experimental psychologists give subjects a long list of words to learn, it is often found that the memory of the first and last words is much better than those in the middle. This is known as 'the bowing effect'. . . . One reason why words in the middle of the list are not remembered so well is that they suffer from proactive and retroactive interference."

67. These are the final lines of Thomas Hood, "Literary Reminiscences," published in the *Comic Annual* for 1833.

68. Anthony Burgess, "Viewpoint," *Times Literary Supplement*, May 11, 1973. Mr. Burgess does not give the couplet which contains his solution.

69. Richard E. Palmer (summarizing Heidegger's view of language), *Hermeneutics* (Evanston, Ill.: Northwestern University Press, 1969), p. 133.

70. The thesis of this and the previous sentence is persuasively argued in Jan M. Meijer, "Verbal Art as Interference," pp. 313–348, esp. p. 329.

71. D. S. Carne-Ross, "Conversation with Robert Lowell," *Delos* 1 (Austin, Texas: National Translation Center, 1968), 169.

72. *Pushkin Threefold*, quotations from Walter Arndt's introduction, pp. xlv, xlvi, xlviii.

73. *Trente-cinq jeunes poètes Américaines*, traduction, préface, et choix par Alain Bosquet (Paris: Gallimard, 1960): Lowell, pp. 324–325; Berryman, pp. 212–213. Bosquet's Lowell also misses any equivalent for "climacteric," which gives paradoxical dignity to the rhyme word "want," which it controls. Robert Lowell's English is quoted from *Life Studies* (New York: Farrar, Straus & Giroux, 1959), p. 88. John Berryman is quoted from his *Short Poems* (New York: Farrar, Straus & Giroux, 1967), p. 114.

74. William McGonagall, "Saving a Train," from *Yet More Comic and Curious Verse*, collected by J. M. Cohen (Harmondsworth: Penguin Books, 1959), p. 117.

75. My thanks to Dr. Judith Saunders for the copy of this poem.

76. The passages quoted are from John Manier, "Tribute to John F. Kennedy," *Primitive Poems* (privately printed, 1966); teenage girl in the comic book *June and Pixie*, London, May 4, 1974.

77. Marianne Moore, *Predilections* (New York: Viking Press, 1955), p. 8.

78. *Collected Poems of Hugh MacDiarmid*, rev. ed. with enlarged glossary prepared by John C. Weston (New York and London: Macmillan, 1967), pp. 320–321.

79. *Letters of Wallace Stevens*, pp. 351–352. The letter dates January 12, 1940.

80. Roger Shattuck's phrase in the introduction to his translation of *Selected Writing of Guillaume Apollinaire* (New York: New Directions, 1971), p. 21. Apollinaire is of the same historical moment as the English and American poets discussed here: to note, with Shattuck, that he "redefined the way in which rimes are masculine and feminine," and that he audaciously rhymes "singulars with plurals, stems with composite forms, words with themselves, and simple component sounds with any vaguely similar sound," is to describe the typical modernist extension, not the abandonment, of the device.

81. W. H. Auden, *Collected Shorter Poems, 1927–1957* (London: Faber and Faber, 1966), p. 229.

82. Kenneth Rexroth, *Collected Shorter Poems* (New York: New Directions, 1966), p. 3.

83. Norman Nicholson, *A Local Habitation* (London: Faber and Faber, 1972), p. 19.

84. "E-Pluribus-Unum," *Chastisement: The Last Poets*, Blue Thumb Records, 1972.

85. Edward Dorn, *Slinger* (Berkeley, Calif.: Wingbow Press, 1975); first passage from the end of "The Cycle," second from the beginning of "Book III of the Winter Book."

86. Viktor Zhirmunski, *Introduction to Metrics: The Theory of Verse*, trans. C. F. Brown, ed. E. Stankiewicz and W. N. Vickery (The Hague-Paris: Mouton, 1968), p. 238 (translation of *Vvedenie e metriku; teoriia stikha* [Leningrad, 1925]).

87. John Logan "The Girl in the Fog," *The Anonymous Lover* (New York: Liverright, 1973), p. 75.

88. Paul Kiparsky "The Role of Linguistics in a Theory of Poetry," *Daedalus* 102, 3 (Summer 1973), 232.

89. W. S. Merwin, *The Carrier of Ladders* (New York: Athenaeum, 1971), p. 50.

90. This is to quote only the transition in the middle of "The Leaden Echo and The Golden Echo," *Poems of Gerard Manley Hopkins*, ed. W. H. Gardner, 3d ed. (London: Oxford University Press, 1964), p. 97.

91. Both quotations from Book I, part ii, W. C. Williams, *Paterson* (New York: New Directions, 1946–1951).

92. James Schuyler, *The Crystal Lithium* (New York: Random House, 1972), pp. 61–62.

93. Recorded, under November 19, 1816, by Benjamin Robert Haydon in his *Autobiography,* ed. Edmund Blunden (Oxford: Oxford University Press, 1927).

3: Modernity and Literary Convention

1. The phrase belongs to David Antin, "Some Questions about Modernism," *Occident* 8, n.s. (Spring 1974), 28. My thanks to William Shu-sam Tay and Ying-hsiung Chou for their information and advice on matters relating to Chinese literature; however any errors in chapter three are solely attributable to me.

2. Feng Chih (b. 1905), from Sonnet XXVII, *The Sonnets,* 1941, English version from *Twentieth Century Chinese Poetry: An Anthology,* trans. and ed. Kai-Yu Hsu (Garden City, New York: Doubleday, 1964), p. 155.

3. Walt Whitman, *Leaves of Grass,* Readers' Edition, ed. Harold W. Bodgett and Sculley Bradley (New York: New York University Press, 1965), p. 714.

4. *Modern Chinese Poetry: Twenty Poets from the Republic of China, 1955–1965,* selected, translated, and with an introduction by Wai-lim Yip (Iowa City: University of Iowa Press, 1967), pp. 49, 65, 104, 129, 152, 168.

5. Ibid., pp. 84, 96.

6. Murray Krieger, "Contextualism and the Relegation of Rhetoric," in Donald C. Bryant, ed., *Rhetoric and Poetic* (Iowa City: University of Iowa Press, 1965), esp. pp. 46–47.

7. S. T. Coleridge, *Shakespearean Criticism,* ed. T. M. Raysor (London: Dent, 1960) I, 197. Though, as Raysor notes, these sentences are "based directly on Schlegel" (p. 197n), this does not render their content any less Coleridgean; Coleridge steals ideas he agrees with.

8. For a hostile account of the concept of organic form, see W. K. Wimsatt, "Organic Form: Some Questions about a Metaphor," in *Day of the Leopards: Essays in Defense of Poems* (New Haven and London: Yale University Press, 1976). On selective organicism in

Wimsatt and the New Critics, see Paul de Man, "Form and Intent in the American New Criticism," in *Blindness and Insight: Essays in the Rhetoric of Contemporary Criticism* (New York: Oxford University Press, 1971).

9. Noam Chomsky, "The Current Scene in Linguistics: Present Directions," in David A. Reibel and Sanford A. Schane, eds., *Modern Studies in English: Readings in Transformational Grammar* (Englewood Cliffs, N.J.: Prentice-Hall, 1969), pp. 10–11.

10. A tentative formulation of a new rhetoric "that would no longer be normative or descriptive but that would more or less openly raise the question of the intentionality of rhetorical figures," is Paul de Man's "The Rhetoric of Temporality," in Charles S. Singleton, ed., *Interpretation: Theory and Practice* (Baltimore: Johns Hopkins University Press, 1969). For a synoptic treatment of French structuralist neorhetoric, see Tzvetan Todorov, *Poétique* (Paris: Seuil, 1973).

11. See Wai-lim Yip, "Yen Yü and the Poetic Theories in the Sung Dynasty," *Tamkang Review* 1, no. 2 (October 1970), esp. 188 on Huang T'ing Chien.

12. Thomas DeQuincey, "Rhetoric," *Collected Writings*, ed. David Masson (London: A. & C. Black, 1897) X, 97.

13. Fredric Jameson, "Criticism in History," in Norman Rudich, ed., *The Weapons of Criticism* (Palo Alto, Calif.: Ramparts Press, 1976), pp. 31–50.

14. Harry Levin, "Notes on Convention," in Harry Levin, ed., *Perspectives of Criticism* (Cambridge, Mass.: Harvard University Press, 1950), p. 73.

15. Claudio Guillén, "A Note on Influences and Conventions," in *Literature as System: Essays Toward the Theory of Literary History* (Princeton, N.J.: Princeton University Press, 1971), pp. 62–65.

16. Leo Ou-fan Lee, *The Romantic Generation of Modern Chinese Writers* (Cambridge, Mass.: Harvard University Press, 1973).

17. Claudio Guillén, "Second Thoughts on Literary Periods," in *Literature as System*, p. 445.

18. Bonnie S. McDougall, *The Introduction of Western Literary Theories into Modern China: 1919–1925* (Tokyo: The Centre for East Asian Cultural Studies, 1971).

19. Chow Tse-tung, *The May Fourth Movement: Intellectual Revolution in Modern China* (Cambridge, Mass.: Harvard University Press, 1960), p. 15.

20. One model for such a theory in the human studies is Thomas S. Kuhn's account of the shifts in research paradigms in the natural sciences; *The Structure of Scientific Revolutions*, 2d ed. enl. (Chicago: University of Chicago Press, 1970).

21. See Geoffrey H. Hartman, *The Unmediated Vision* (New Haven: Yale University Press, 1954).

22. Gérard Genette, *Figures I* (Paris: Seuil, 1966), pp. 262–263; my translation.

23. Further attested by the title of a new journal, *boundary 2, a journal of postmodern literature*, Binghamton. Presumably the second boundary is the new historical break that divides modernism from its aftermath.

24. Roland Barthes, *Elements of Semiology*, trans. A. Lavers and C. Smith (London: Cape, 1967), pp. 86–88. See also, on this break between classical and modern writing, Barthes's *Writing Degree Zero*, trans. A. Lavers and C. Smith (London: Cape, 1967), passim, and *Mythologies*, trans. A. Lavers (London: Paladin, 1972), esp. pp. 133–134.

25. W. B. Yeats, *Autobiography* (New York: Macmillan, 1953), p. 94.

26. A. Alvarez, *The Savage God* (New York: Random House, 1972), p. 17.

27. In Stephen Berg and Robert Mezey, eds., *Naked Poetry: Recent American Poetry in Open Forms* (Indianapolis: Bobbs-Merrill, 1969), p. 270.

28. Wen I-to, *Twentieth Century Chinese Poetry*, pp. 65–66.

29. For notions in this sentence and several other details in this paragraph I have relied on Cyril Birch, "English and Chinese Meters in Hsü Chih-mo's Poetry," *Asia Major*, n.s., 8, part 2 (1961), 258–293, esp. 276–279.

30. Birch (ibid., p. 277) introduces full English syntax in his literal translation: "But scraps of brass may hue to turquoise (sic), / Peach-blossoms flower from rusting cans, / The greasy scum weave a texture of gauze / And a tinted haze steam up from the germs." Though I cannot accept Birch's application of English metrical terminology to Chinese (usually it does not explain English verse; how much less helpful with Chinese!), I have adopted his division of syllables because it has its origin in remarks of Wen I-to himself. Literal translation of Chinese characters, with transliterations above, kindly supplied to me by Ying-hsiung Chou.

31. Wen I-to is quoted in Kai-Yu Hsu, "The Life and Poetry of Wen I-to," *Harvard Journal of Asiatic Studies* 21 (1958), 134–179; see p. 151.

32. Paul de Man, "Literary History and Literary Modernity," in *Blindness and Insight: Essays in the Rhetoric of Contemporary Criticism* (New York: Oxford University Press, 1971), p. 144.

33. See, for definitions of terms, Robert Abernathy, "Rhymes, Non-Rhymes, and Antirhyme," in *To Honor Roman Jakobson: Essays on the Occasion of his Seventieth Birthday*, (The Hague-Paris: Mouton, 1967), 1:1–14.

34. *Selected Poems of H.D.* [Hilda Doolittle] (New York: Grove Press, 1957), p. 26.

35. Gottfried von Neifen, ca. 1240, first three lines of poem xxxii (five stanzas), in C. v. Kraus, *Deutsche Liederdichter des 13. Jahrhunderts*, bd. 1; text (Tuebingen, 1952), p. 115 f. My thanks to Martin Wierschim for advice on these MHG texts.

36. Walter von der Vogelweide, poem L47, lines 16–21, in K. Lachmann, C. v. Kraus, H. Kuhn, *Die Gedichte Walthers von der Vogelweide* (Berlin, 1965), p. 66.

37. Gottfried von Neifen, ca. 1235, poem v in Kraus, *Deutsche Liederdichter*, p. 87 f. This is the complete second stanza of a five stanza poem.

38. *Roman de la rose*, XX, 955. Quoted by Pierre Guiraud, *Les sources médiévales de la poésie formelle: la rime* (Groningen: J. B. Wolters, 1952), p. 20. This inaugural lecture can also be found in Guiraud's *Essais de stylistique* (Paris: Klincksieck, 1969).

39. Quoted from *Leys d'Amors*, by Guiraud, *Les sources médiévales*, p. 21.

40. Ibid., this and the next quotation from p. 3.

41. Henry Lanz, *The Physical Basis of Rime An Essay on the Aesthetics of Sound* (Stanford, Stanford University Press, 1931), p. 55.

42. T. S. Eliot, *The Waste Land*, lines 117–124, in *The Complete Poems and Plays* (New York: Harcourt, Brace, 1964), pp. 40–41.

43. D. H. Lawrence, "Bavarian Gentians," in *The Poems of D. H. Lawrence*, collected and edited with an introduction and notes by Vivian de Sola Pinto and Warren Roberts (New York: Viking Press, 1964), 2:697.

44. Hugh Kenner, *The Pound Era* (Berkeley, Los Angeles, London: University of California Press, 1971), p. 93.

45. Robert Creeley, *For Love, Poems 1950–1960* (New York: Charles Scribner's and Sons, 1962), p. 79.

46. *Mercian Hymns* is printed in full in Geoffrey Hill's *Somewhere is Such a Kingdom: Poems 1952–1971* (Boston: Houghton Mifflin, 1971).

47. Calvin Bedient, *Eight Contemporary Poets* (London: Oxford University Press, 1974), p. x.

48. Josephine Miles, *Prefabrications* (Bloomington: Indiana University Press, 1955), p. 47.

49. Juri Tynjanov and Roman Jakobson, "Les problèmes des études littéraires et linguistiques," in *Théorie de la littérature*, trans. Tzvetan Todorov (Paris: Seuil, 1965), pp. 138–139: my translation.

50. This is the final stanza of Philip Larkin's "Money," *High Windows* (London: Faber and Faber, 1974).

51. From the third of Davie's "Six Epistles to Eva Hesse," *Collected Poems* (London: Routledge, 1972), pp. 260–261. "And now's the time / To venture a Defense of Rhyme" begins a long section which argues that rule keeping in rhyme "makes the rhymed forms open ones," while "Total freedom in the fiction / Is of all the worst constriction."

52. *Robert Bridges: Poetry and Prose*, ed. John Sparrow (Oxford: Oxford University Press, 1955), pp. 123–124.

53. E. E. Cummings, "POEM, OR BEAUTY HURTS MR. VINAL," *Poems: 1923–1954* (New York: Harcourt, Brace, 1954), pp. 167–168.

54. Rhyme, and "meter as meter and not as the essential of the work, one of its words," Williams considered as "complicated ritualistic forms designed to separate the work from 'reality'": W. C. Williams, *Spring and All* (West Newbury, Mass.: Frontier Press, 1971), p. 23. And yet, carefully, Williams used rhyme; see below for instances from *Paterson*.

55. George Saintsbury, *History of English Prosody*, vol. 3, appendix iv, "Rhyme, 1600–1900" (London, 1910; reprinted, New York: Russell & Russell, 1961), p. 539.

56. "Scenting in every corner the chances of rhyme" (line 6) Charles Baudelaire, "Le Soleil," *Oeuvres complètes*, texte établi et annoté par Y-G. Le Dantec (Paris: Gallimard, 1954), p. 155; my italics. Walter Benjamin's study is titled *Charles Baudelaire: A Lyric Poet in the Era of High Capitalism*, trans. Harry Zohn (London: New Left Books, 1973).

57. Charles Tomlinson, *The Way of a World* (Oxford: Oxford University Press, 1969), p. 59.

Conclusion

1. W. Jackson Bate, *The Burden of the Past and the English Poet* (Cambridge, Mass.: Harvard University Press, 1970); and Harold Bloom, *The Anxiety of Influence: A Theory of Poetry* (New York: Oxford University Press, 1973).

2. Paul de Man "Form and Intent in the American New Criticism," in *Blindness and Insight: Essays in the Rhetoric of Contemporary Criticism* (New York: Oxford University Press, 1971), p. 25.

3. Quoted from E. D. Hirsch, Jr., *Validity in Interpretation* (New Haven and London: Yale University Press, 1967), p. 32.

4. Graham Hough, *An Essay on Criticism* (London: Duckworth, 1966), p. 158.

5. One might propose the usefulness of a book that would study not so much particular forms as the idea of forming since, say, 1660 —with chapters describing several phenomena of an era of stylistic pluralism after 1795, including sprung rhythm, the prose poem, and the prosodies of free verse.

6. Henri Meschonnic, *Pour la poétique: Essai* (Paris: Gallimard, 1970), p. 30; my translation.

7. New Critics on Longinus: Allen Tate, "Longinus and the 'New Criticism,'" in *The Man of Letters in the Modern World* (New York: Meridian Books, 1955), pp. 175–192; W. K. Wimsatt, Jr., and Cleanth Brooks, "Roman Classicism: Longinus," in *Literary Criticism: A Short History* (New York: Knopf, 1966), pp. 99–111. Both these books are sustained meditations on the evils of expressionism. A response to such a position, especially as found in the aesthetic theories of W. K. Wimsatt's frequent collaborator Monroe Beardsley, may be found in Guy V. Sircillo, *Mind and Art: An Essay on the Varieties of Expression* (Princeton, N.J.: Princeton University Press, 1972).

8. Marx W. Wartofsky, "Art As Humanizing Praxis," *Praxis* I, 1 (Spring 1975), 60.

9. Raymond Williams, "Base and Superstructure in Marxist Cultural Theory," *New Left Review* 82 (November-December 1973), 15.

10. The quotation is from Murray Krieger, *A Window to Criticism* (Princeton, N.J.: Princeton University Press, 1964), p. 57.

Selected Bibliography

DEVICE

Ambrogio, Ignazio. *Formalismo e avanguardia in Russia.* Roma: Editori Riuniti, 1968.

Bann, Stephen, compiler. *Russian Formalism.* Edinburgh: Scottish Academic Press, 1973.

Barthes, Roland. *Elements of Semiology.* Translated by A. Lavers and C. Smith. London: Cape, 1967.

Burckhardt, Sigurd. "The Poet as Fool and Priest." In *Shakespearean Meanings.* Princeton, N.J.: Princeton University Press, 1968.

Burke, Kenneth. *Counter-Statement.* 2d ed. Los Altos, Calif.: Hermes, 1953.

Erlich, Victor, *Russian Formalism: History-Doctrine.* 2d ed. The Hague-Paris: Mouton, 1965.

Fowler, Alastair. "The Selection of Literary Constructs." *New Literary History* 7, 1 (Autumn 1975), 39–55.

Fussell, Edwin. *Lucifer in Harness: American Meter, Metaphor, and Diction.* Princeton, N.J.: Princeton University Press, 1973.

Fussell, Paul, Jr. *Poetic Meter and Poetic Form.* New York: Random House, 1965.

Genette, Gérard. *Figures I.* Paris: Seuil, 1966.

———. *Figures II.* Paris: Seuil, 1969.

Jakobson, Roman. "Linguistics and Poetics." In *Style in Langauge.* Edited by Thomas A. Sebeok. Cambridge, Mass.: M.I.T. Press, 1960. Pp. 350–377.

———. *Questions de poétique.* Paris: Seuil, 1973.

Jameson, Fredric. *The Prison-House of Language: A Critical Account of Structuralism and Russian Formalism.* Princeton, N.J.: Princeton University Press, 1972.

Kibedy Varga, A. *Les constantes du poème.* La Haye: 1963.

Kiparsky, Paul. "The Role of Linguistics in a Theory of Poetry," *Daedalus* (Summer 1973), pp. 231–244.

La Drière, Craig. "Structure, Sound and Meaning." In *Sound and Poetry.* Edited by Northrop Frye. New York: Columbia University Press, 1957. Pp. 85–108.

Leech, Geoffrey N. *A Linguistic Guide to English Poetry.* London: Longmans, 1969.

Lemon, Lee T., and Marion J. Reis. *Russian Formalist Criticism.* Lincoln: University of Nebraska Press, 1965.

Levin, Harry. "Notes on Convention." *Perspectives of Criticism.* Edited by Harry Levin. Cambridge, Mass.: Harvard University Press, 1950.

Levý, Jiří. "The Meanings of Form and the Forms of Meaning." *Poetics-Poetyka-Poetika II.* Warsaw: Mouton with Polish Scientific Publishers, 1966. Pp. 45–59.

Lohner, Edgar. "The Intrinsic Method: Some Reconsiderations." In *The Disciplines of Criticism: Essays in Literary Theory, and History.* Edited by P. Demetz, T. Greene, and L. Nelson, Jr. New Haven and London: Yale University Press, 1968.

Lotman, Juri. *La Structure du texte artistique.* Traduit du Russe. Préface d'Henri Meschonnic. Paris: Gallimard, 1973; Moscow, 1970.

Matejka, Ladislav, and Krystyna Pomorska. *Readings in Russian Poetics: Formalist and Structuralist Views.* Cambridge, Mass.: M.I.T. Press, 1971.

Meijer, Jan M. "Literature as Information: Some Notes on Lotman's Book," and "Verbal Art as Interference Between a Cognitive and an Aesthetic Structure." In *Structure of Texts and Semiotics of Culture.* Edited by Jan van der Eng and Mojmír Grygar. The Hague-Paris: Mouton, 1973.

Meschonnic, Henri. *Pour la poétique: essai.* Paris: Gallimard, 1970.

Poggioli, Renato. "Poetics and Metrics." In *Comparative Literature.* Proceedings of the Second Congress of the International Comparative Literature Association. Edited by Werner P. Friedrich. Chapel Hill: University of North Carolina Press, 1959. Pp. 192–203.

Pomorska, Krystyna. *Russian Formalist Theory and Its Poetic Ambience.* The Hague-Paris: Mouton, 1968.

Smith, Barbara Herrnstein. *Poetic Closure: A Study of How Poems End.* Chicago: University of Chicago Press, 1968.

Thompson, Ewa M. *Russian Formalism and Anglo-American New Criticism: A Comparative Study.* The Hague-Paris: Mouton, 1971.

Todorov, Tzvetan, trans. *Théorie de la littérature: textes des Formalistes Russes.* Paris: Seuil, 1965.

Wellek, René, and Austin Warren. "Euphony, Rhythm, and Meter." Chapter 13 of *Theory of Literature.* New York: Harcourt, Brace, 1949.

Welsh, Andrew. *Roots of Lyric: Primitive Poetry and Modern Poetics.* Princeton, N.J.: Princeton University Press, 1978.

Wimsatt, W. K. *The Verbal Icon: Studies in the Meaning of Poetry.* Lexington: University of Kentucky Press, 1954.

———. *Hateful Contraries: Studies in Literature and Criticism.* Lexington: University of Kentucky Press, 1965.

———. *Day of the Leopards: Essays in Defense of Poems.* New Haven and London: Yale University Press, 1976.

MODERNITY

Antin, David. "Some Questions About Modernism." In *Occident,* n.s., 7 (Spring 1974), 7–38.

Barthes, Roland. *Writing Degree Zero.* Translated by A. Lavers and C. Smith. London: Cape, 1967.

Bate, W. Jackson. *The Burden of the Past and the English Poet.* Cambridge, Mass.: Harvard University Press, 1970.

Bloom, Harold. *The Anxiety of Influence: A Theory of Poetry.* New York: Oxford University Press, 1973.

———. *A Map of Misreading.* New York: Oxford University Press, 1975.

———. *Kabbalah and Criticism.* New York: Seabury Press, 1975.

Calinescu, Matei. *Faces of Modernity: Avant-Garde, Decadence, Kitsch.* Bloomington and London: Indiana University Press, 1977.

Guillén, Claudio. *Literature as System: Essays Toward the Theory of Literary History.* Princeton, N.J.: Princeton University Press, 1971.

Jameson, Fredric. *Marxism and Form: Twentieth-Century Dialectical Theories of Literature.* Princeton, N.J.: Princeton University Press, 1971.

———. "Beyond the Cave: Demystifying the Ideology of Modernism." *Bulletin of the Midwest Modern Language Association 8,* 1 (Spring 1975), 1–20.

———. "Criticism in History." In *The Weapons of Criticism.* Edited by Norman Rudich. Palo Alto, Calif.: Ramparts Press, 1976. Pp. 31–50.

de Man, Paul. "Literary History and Literary Modernity." In his *Blindness and Insight: Essays in the Rhetoric of Contemporary Criticism.* New York: Oxford University Press, 1971.

Meyer, Leonard. *Music, the Arts, and Ideas.* Chicago: University of Chicago Press, 1967.

Miles, Josephine. *Poetry and Change: Donne, Milton, Wordsworth and the Equilibrium of the Present.* Berkeley, Los Angeles, London: University of California Press, 1974.

Paz, Octavio. *Children of the Mire: Modern Poetry from Romanticism to the Avant-Garde.* Translated by Rachel Phillips. Cambridge, Mass.: Harvard University Press, 1974.

Poggioli, Renato. *The Theory of the Avant-Garde.* Translated by Gerald Fitzgerald. Cambridge, Mass.: Harvard University Press, 1968.

Trilling, Lionel. *Sincerity and Authenticity.* Cambridge, Mass.: Harvard University Press, 1973.

Rhyme

Abernathy, Robert. "Rhymes, Non-Rhymes, and Antirhyme." In *To Honor Roman Jakobson: Essays on the Occasion of his Seventieth Birthday.* The Hague-Paris: Mouton, 1967. Pp. 1–14.

Bollinger, Dwight L. "Rime, Assonance, and Morpheme Analysis." *Word 7,* 2 (August 1950), 117–136.

Brecht, Bertolt. "On Rhymeless Verse with Irregular Rhythms." In *Brecht on Theatre.* Edited and translated by John Willett. New York: Hill & Wang, 1964.

Campion, Thomas. *Observations in the Art of English Poesie.* London, 1602.

Daniel, Samuel. *A Defence of Ryme.* London, 1603.

Draper, J. W. "The Origin of Rhyme." *Revue de la littérature comparée* 1 (1957), 74–85.

Eekman, Thomas. *The Realm of Rime: A Study of Rime in the Poetry of the Slavs.* Amsterdam: Hakkert, 1974.

Eliot, T. S. "Reflections on *Vers Libre.*" In his *To Criticize the Critic.* New York: Farrar, Straus & Giroux, 1965.

Guggenheimer, Eva H. *Rhyme Effects and Rhyming Figures: A Comparative Study of Sound Repetitions in the Classics with Emphasis on Latin Poetry.* The Hague-Paris: Mouton, 1972.

Guiraud, Pierre. "Les sources médiévales de la poésie formelle: la rime." In his *Essais de stylistique.* Paris: Klincksieck, 1969. Pp. 245–263.

Hartman, Geoffrey. "The Voice of the Shuttle: Language From the Point of View of Literature." In his *Beyond Formalism: Literary Essays, 1958–1970.* New Haven and London: Yale University Press, 1970.

Hollander, John. *Vision and Resonance: Two Senses of Poetic Form.* New York: Oxford University Press, 1975.

Hopkins, Gerard Manley. "Rhetoric and the Other Structural Parts of Rhetoric—Verse" and "Poetry and Verse." In *The Journals and Papers of Gerard Manley Hopkins.* Edited by Humphrey House, completed by Graham Storey. London: Oxford University Press, 1959.

Kenner, Hugh, "Pope's Reasonable Rhymes." ELH 41, 1 (Spring 1974).

Lanz, Henry. *The Physical Basis of Rime: An Essay on the Aesthetics of Sound.* Stanford, Calif.: Stanford University Press, 1931.

Miller, J. Hillis. Chapter on Gerard Manley Hopkins, especially pp. 277–284. In his *The Disappearance of God.* Cambridge, Mass.: Harvard University Press, 1965.

Pendlebury, B. J. *The Art of the Rhyme.* New York: Scribners, 1971.

Perloff, Marjorie. *Rhyme and Meaning in the Poetry of Yeats.* 's-Gravenhage: Mouton, 1970.

Preminger, Alex, ed. *Encyclopedia of Poetry and Poetics.* Princeton, N.J.: Princeton University Press, 1965. (The article on rhyme, pp. 705–710, is by Arthur Melville Clark and Harold Whitehall.)

Richardson, Charles F. *A Study of English Rhyme.* Hanover, N.H.: printed for classroom use, 1909.

Rickey, Mary Ellen. *Rhyme and Meaning in Richard Crashaw.* Lexington, Ky.: University of Kentucky Press, 1961.

Saintsbury, George. *History of English Prosody.* 3 vols. London: 1910.

Schütze, J. S. *Versuch einer Theorie des Reimes nach Inhalt und Form.* 1802.

Shapiro, Michael. "Sémiotique de la rime." *Poétique* 20 (1974).

———. *Asymmetry: An Inquiry into the Linguistic Structure of Poetry.* Amsterdam: North-Holland Publishing Company, 1976.

Shipley, Joseph T. *Dictionary of World Literature: Criticism-Forms-Technique.* New York: Philosophical Library, 1943. (The entries on rhyme are by Henry Lanz and Thomas Walter Herbert.)

Whitehall, Harold. "From Linguistics to Poetry." In *Sound and Poetry.* Edited by Northrop Frye. New York: Columbia University Press, 1957.

Wimsatt, W. K. "One Relation of Rhyme to Reason." In his *The Verbal Icon: Studies in the Meaning of Poetry.* Lexington, Ky.: University of Kentucky Press, 1954.

Wyld, Henry Cecil. *English Rhyme from Surrey to Pope.* London, 1923; reprinted., New York: Russell & Russell, 1965.

Zhirmunski, Viktor. *Rifma, ee istorija i teorija* [*Rhyme: Its History and Theory*]. Voprosy poètiki 3. Petersburg: Academia, 1923.

Index